COMMUNITY EDUCATORS

A Resource for Educating and Developing Our Youth

By Patricia Moore Harbour
Foreword by David Mathews

KETTERING
FOUNDATION
PRESS

Research Associate:	Amshatar Monroe
Editors:	Margie Loyacano
	Melinda Gilmore
Copy Editor:	Lisa Boone-Berry
Design and Production:	Long's Graphic Design, Inc.

Community Educators: A Resource for Educating and Developing Our Youth is published by the Kettering Foundation Press. The interpretations and conclusions contained in this book represent the views of the author. They do not necessarily reflect the views of the Charles F. Kettering Foundation, its directors, or its officers.

For information about permission to reproduce selections from this book, write to:

> Permissions
> Kettering Foundation Press
> 200 Commons Road
> Dayton, Ohio 45459

This book is printed on acid-free paper.

First edition, 2012

Manufactured in the United States of America

ISBN: 978-0-923993-44-3

Library of Congress Control Number: 2012940361

This book is dedicated to Payton, Christopher, Cameron, and Camden, my grandsons. May you be always nurtured, developed, and educated in a culture of learning that supports you and facilitates you to become wise leaders and the confident, caring, competent, contributing, citizens you are destined to be.

—Your very own,
Gigi

ACKNOWLEDGEMENTS

The beauty of writing a book is the journey and what is encountered along the way. Although, what is to be written is clear, there are many branches bearing fruit. Choices must be made to stay on course. The best learning is experiential so, when I choose a branch that is interesting and valuable but does not serve the purpose, I return to the path, note what has been learned, make a course correction if necessary, and continue the journey. With each step, each quarter turn, there is a deeper wisdom and knowledge that emerges and the author's life, my life, is enriched. I am deeply grateful to the Kettering Foundation and to its president, David Mathews, whose commitment to the relationship between democracy, education, and communities initiated the inquiry that gave birth to the Community Educators Research Initiative and the publication of this book. I thank John Dedrick for guidance and steadfast support.

I am grateful to Carolyn Farrow-Garland for our collaborative partnership in planning and convening the research conversations and for her commitment and confidence in me to shape the study.

Many thanks to Maxine Thomas; I am deeply indebted to her for managing and moving the book to final publication. Maxine, along with her very capable assistant, Bettina Wright, have been an incredible support to me.

I would also like to thank the members of the Kettering Foundation's Public-Public Education Work Group, 2007-2010, for their resourcefulness, considered reflection, and candor. Our monthly meetings were a space for learning, inquiry, and suggestions that challenged my thinking and yielded support for planning, clarity, and execution of the initiative. Special thanks to Connie Crockett, who convened the first group of community educators, and to Randy Nielsen, whose wise questions always provoke quality conversation. Thank you to Libby Kingseed, with whom I collaborated in the research conversations and who provided source documents needed for this publication. Many thanks to Amy Lee, Dorothy Battle, Ileana Marin, and Phil Lurie for their thoughts and encouragement.

I appreciate Paloma Dallas for her assistance with the publication, including listening and reacting to the development of the context and for providing requested resources, text, and references. Also, Amelia Law, a jewel, worked closely with me. She made sure handouts, reports, agendas, logistics, and preparations for the research conversations were successfully coordinated.

Thanks to Lara Rusch, Angie Allen, and Alexandra Robinson. Each helped document the research conversations. Alexandra helped enormously with analysis and interpretation of this information. Foday Sulimani and Moshood Folorunsho also participated in several Community Educators research conversations.

The contributions, support, and encouragement of colleague and Kettering associate David Brown has been awesome. He and I collaborated at many levels throughout the research conversations. He contributed articles for discussion, as well as his knowledge of the work of education historian Lawrence Cremin, whose broader view of education influenced the purpose for this research. I appreciate and thank my many other Kettering colleagues who tirelessly contributed their support to ensure that administrative matters and logistics for the study and the book were handled efficiently. Lane Wells handled all travel arrangements; Marie Sims, Margaret Dixon, Glenda Rose, Angel George, Kathy Heil, and Nancy Dougherty—always full of encouragement and a sense of humor—made sure I had the necessary tools and supplies. Nellie Click and Rita Shanesy took extra care to make sure the fiscal matters were managed with excellence. Mindy Fogt and Eric Ellcessor graciously provided the computer hardware, accessories, and software I needed for greater efficiency in the office. They also recorded our research conversations and provided transcripts.

It is with much appreciation and gratitude that I acknowledge and thank the citizen educators with whom I worked and learned from to produce this report about their remarkable work. I thank each participant in the research conversations and the respondents who completed the online survey. I appreciate the openness with which they shared what, why, and how they do what they do, as well as their achievements and challenges. This book could not have been written without the contributions of the individuals and the organizations and communities they represent. Thank you ... Rachel Antrobus, Leon Andrews, Karen Atkins, Atum Azzahir, Nance Bell, Carol Blackman, Michael Blowen, Mary K. Boyd, Matt Bradley, Katrina Brink, Kevin Brown, Everett Browning, Stephanie Burch, Caitlin Cahill, Cindy Carlson, Frank Chisley, Becky Cooper, Bob Cornett, George Crawley, Mitzi Downing, Dave Farley, Bridget Gothberg, James Graves, Cindy Guyton, Judy Heyboer, Sara L. Hill, Carlenia (Jackie) Jackson, Sheila Jackson, Kathy Johnson, Catherine Jordan, Jackie Kennedy, Pam King, Shannon McCartney-Simper, Merle McGee, Michael McSurdy, Esther Mota, Bruce Mundy, Francisco Nunez, William O'Callaghan, Beth Offenbacker, Rev. Kathy O'Keeffe, Pastor Tony Ortiz, J. J. Pitman, Bonnie Politz, David Quijada, Sharon Richardson, Christine Sartin, Joyce Spicer, Ann Stiles, Troy Strothers, Mindy Sturm, Nancy Tellett-Royce, Tiffany Mitchell Thomas, Linda Thornton, Susanna Thornton, Marsha Timpson, Morrell Todd, Sharon Walker, Catherine Warner, Donyata Washington, Tom Widlowski, and Wendy Wheeler.

A very special thanks goes to Mary K. Boyd, Becky Cooper, Kathy Johnson, Patrick Johnson, Phil Stewart, and Ann Stiles for the inspiring stories they contributed specifically for this book. Caitlin Cahill, whom I interviewed, graciously shared information, research, and publications, developed and written by her and her colleagues, Matt Bradley, David Quijada, and her students. The stories and thoughts they contributed reflect some of the amazing accomplishments young people are making in their communities, as they bring about social, political, and civic change. I am grateful to survey respondents who contributed compelling stories from their program experiences. The identities of respondents in the survey remain anonymous, but participants in the research conversations gave permission for their identities and comments in those conversations to be shared.

I owe a great deal of appreciation to Sharon Newbill of Folkstone: Evaluation Anthropology, who completed the analysis of the Community Educators Survey and provided an exceptionally informative report and interpretation of that data.

I have saved until now the outstanding partners who contributed many long hours on this project to ensure this book was ready for printing and distribution. I am eternally indebted to my editing team; Margie Loyacano, for the outstanding editing that supported me as I crafted the words and shaped the book. Margie's suggestions were invaluable for me, better illuminating intended meaning and clearly communicating the essence of the work. I am grateful to Margie for her absolutely essential role. Lisa Boone-Berry, copy editor, a wonderful spirit, and awesome talent, reviewed, edited, and proofed to be certain that every word, to the last, did its job. Much thanks and appreciation to Melinda Gilmore, review editor for the Kettering Foundation, who was magnificent in scrutinizing the final copy for accuracy and for consistency with the over-all Kettering research. Their support and encouragement has been worth its weight in gold.

There are no words to express my deep gratitude to Amshatar Monroe, outstanding researcher, consultant, and friend on the journey. She did far more than assist with the research; she read with me, listened and recorded my words, challenged my thinking, offered her wisdom, managed details, checking and rechecking as requested. She inspired me to bring more of my passion and years of experience in education to this work.

Steve Long, an excellent graphic artist, seemed to grasp what I wanted from our first conversation. His illustrations and layout exceeded my expectations. I am grateful to Steve not only for the talent and quality he brought to this project, but for the professionalism that characterizes his demeanor.

In the end, nearly every author completes his or her book with the personal support of family and friends. My team has been outstanding throughout this journey. They understood when I could not stop working or return phone calls and when I missed events I otherwise would not have missed. They rejoiced with me in those "aha" moments. They have been my cheerleaders and a source of encouragement and motivation. I especially want to thank my daughters, Lisa Harbour Carter and Wenda K. Harbour, who I can always count on to support and encourage me; Juanita Doss Burrell, Flossie Reed, Goldie Bryant, and Evelyn "Jimmy" Johnson, who were excellent sounding boards with candid feedback. Jimmy often brought lunch. Also, many thanks to Paris Brown, my special teenage "niece" who read with me, and to Misty Frost, who took time to type one of the first documents that reported on this project. And finally, special gratitude goes to Leon Pace who has been a daily support, and who proofed drafts, challenged my thinking, made special treats, and made sure I had the space I needed to focus and write.

TABLE OF CONTENTS

FOREWORD

INTRODUCING COMMUNITY EDUCATORS

by David Mathews

Concerns about what public schools aren't doing, or aren't able to do, are too well known to repeat them here. Although always mindful of the importance of schools, Kettering Foundation has also been pursuing a related issue: given the concerns about the public school system, are people taking steps to supplement what the schools are doing? And if this is happening, who is doing it and what are they doing? Is something new occurring that's different from the services provided by Boys & Girls Clubs of America, Little League Baseball and Softball, and tutorial programs? (These are all helpful, but they've been around for some time.) At the foundation, we are trying to find out whether there are new "community educators" who are using local resources to strengthen students' ability to learn. If there are such educators, how do they go about doing their work, especially if it requires getting other people to join them?

This book does not answer all of Kettering's questions; still, we have learned a great deal from the large and diverse group of community educators that Pat Harbour brought to the foundation to talk about their efforts. For instance, we are impressed by the variety of local resources community educators are using to educate. The resources range from community history to art. And the classrooms are places like fire stations and theaters. (Jack Shelton describes other local resources being used to educate in a NewSouth Books publication, *Consequential Learning: A Public Approach to Better Schools*.) We also learned that citizens started their programs less out of frustration with the schools and more out of concern with family instability, youth violence, or simply the lack of opportunity to learn essential life skills.

The foundation is especially interested in how these community educators do what they do. We are struck by differences between the stories we first heard about how programs were started and those told in later meetings. Initially, the stories centered on a single leader who stepped out front and began a project. Yet as the people meeting with us became more reflective, their stories were more about people joining forces to carry out a collaborative project. We want to find out more about how community educators decide what to do, how they identify resources, and whether they act with others in ways that are mutually reinforcing.

Kettering's research generally has to do with how people come together to act when they sense something is going wrong or not getting done yet haven't agreed on what the problem is or what to do about it. For example, people know that they want kids to be successful, but they aren't sure how to make that happen. Citizens also differ over what is the right thing to do, and no one group of people or one institution, the schools, can solve a problem alone. The most serious problems that threaten young people's success are often of this sort. And that overworked phrase, *it takes a village*, turns out to be right on target. Communities that seem to be doing the best job of preparing young people are communities where, as was said in one city, "everybody is trying to teach these kids." So Kettering looks very closely at community programs that involve a number of citizens and have the potential to inspire others to start their own programs.

We look especially at who identifies the problem or the need to be met. Who gets to say what the problem is? And if there is more than one option or course of action for solving the problem (and there usually is), are all the options considered fairly? If there is disagreement over which option is best (and that, too, is common), is the disagreement addressed and worked through? *How* a decision is made can be as important as *what* the decision is. Then there is the matter of implementing the decision. How are resources identified? After all, many of the community resources used in the programs described in this book are different from the resources professional educators use. And once the resources are identified and committed, if there are multiple programs or multiple tasks in a single project, how are they organized? Do the efforts complement or reinforce one another, leading to maximum effectiveness? Most important, we would like to know what community educators learn as they go about their work. Do they move toward a fixed goal and use quantitative measures to evaluate their progress, or do they reevaluate their objectives as they go along? Do they try to learn as much about how they work together as what they accomplish?

If the ideal is for everyone to use the resources at their disposal to educate, and if education does indeed take a village, then the answers we can get to these questions from the efforts of community educators can move us closer to that ideal. The foundation is pleased to share its first look at community educators. Their programs are impressive in themselves and, taken together, they suggest that the community itself can be an educational institution.

While schools have been, and will continue to be, our primary institutions for instructing the next generation, Americans have always used a variety of means to educate the young. With the invention of new communications technologies, there will certainly be more ways found to educate. These may not all be "high tech," however. Some of these new means of educating may be familiar—even old-fashioned—and the resources they draw on may be close-at-hand, awaiting only the imagination of a new generation of community educators to recognize and use them.

David Mathews is president of the
Charles F. Kettering Foundation,
former president of The University
of Alabama, and former secretary of the
US Department of Health, Education,
and Welfare.

PREFACE

Who Educates Our Youth? *Community Educators: A Resource for Educating and Developing Our Youth* asserts that education is broader than just schooling. It recognizes that the relationship between education, democracy, and community is inseparable. This book illustrates the important lessons learned from citizens, organizations, and communities dedicated to the development of youth. The findings reported here are drawn from Kettering Foundation community educators research conducted between 2007-2010.

The intention is to heighten consciousness and renew passion to establish ownership and responsibility for *all* young people, their education, their growth, and their development. This book is a "call for collaboration and action." *In what ways is your community a resource for educating and developing youth? How do you connect and collaborate with others to make the seminal difference for every young person to achieve academically and develop into a productive and contributive citizen?* Consider also the deeper questions: *How does your community shift the current paradigm, which focuses predominantly on changing schools, to a broader view that transforms education? How does your community ensure an environment that is advantageous for all young people to grow, learn, and develop to their highest potential?*

In every reference to the community, schools and the school district are deemed to be an integral part and a subset of the whole, not a separate entity. Businesses and other sectors, residents in all neighborhoods, elected officials, local government, service agencies, museums, and other organizations comprise the collective community; all are vital to pave the way for young people.

Why Does This Book Matter?

Community Educators sets as a challenge the need to view education as broader than the current accepted thinking and to act on improving education through collaborative relationships. And yes, it does matter that people's futures and the viability of communities are fundamentally linked to the prospects and consequences youth may encounter. Beyond this, however, the ideas in this publication are a reminder that, in a democracy, the public is responsible for education. And in today's environment in which education continues to appear as a political "football," this book is timely, calling attention to personal and collective responsibility to improve education. Furthermore, you are invited to make the distinction between change that is systemic and sustainable over time and education improvements that are later challenged and discarded as circumstances are altered.

Even today, after 30-40 years of modifications intended to "improve" education, our nation, our youth, and our democracy are *still* at risk. The myriad improvements, new requirements, and research targeted to correct education problems are heavily weighted toward expecting schools and districts to "fix it."

It is important to remember that we cannot expect a different result using the same approach. Outcries from every corner of this nation express a concern that education must be improved. But, in reality, the common cry is actually "fix these schools."

Community Educators asks you to examine your perspective in the face of a possible new reality that moves beyond blame and shame and, instead, pleads for collaboration. Examine carefully what and who in your community can and do educate and develop young people. And underlying all of this is a question to consider: In a democratic society, should schools continue to be expected to do this alone? If not, or if so, what does this mean for your community?

How to Use This Book

In this book, I share my personal and professional stories and real experiences to build a connection from an earlier time when citizens, professional educators, and parents were the "villagers" who shared in the education process. These "villagers" were involved in encouraging youth to aspire to a prosperous and productive future. They were also partners in shaping social and character development. These stories are discussed in detail throughout the book. A "Story from the Field" is featured between each chapter. This is a story written or shared by a youth, program director, or a community educator.

To build a foundation for establishing a framework and launching point that connects the past to the present, Chapters 1 and 2 share stories and discuss views and theories of outstanding education historians and scholars to illustrate pertinent themes. These scholars and many others have had remarkable influence and success for improving schools. Also, a clarifying distinction is made between what it means to transform education or to reform schools.

Chapters 3, 4, and 5 focus on Kettering research on community educators. In chapter 3, community educators, in their own words and stories, describe their programs, who educates, and what and why they do what they do. Chapter 4 describes the challenges and obstacles encountered by the various programs. The findings and lessons learned from the study and the online survey that was administered in the study are described in Chapter 5. The full report interpreting the survey analysis may be found in the Appendix. Finally, Chapter 6 discusses possible implications for further study and your consideration. At the end of Chapter 6, all the questions presented for reflection and possible community discussion are provided, for your convenience, in one place.

You may find it helpful to approach each page with an open, inquiring mind. Become part of the narrative, interact with the book, and reflect on the questions. Generate your own questions, taking into account your community and including your schools. Recall your own stories that connect with stories and experiences presented. And finally, use this book to generate conversations with other members of your community.

In writing this book I was amazed by an unexpected discovery. There is a common principle with which the community educators, teachers, and scholars agree is important to educate and develop youth. This principle is a belief that has always captured my imagination. I was reminded that for decades teachers, including me, applied this principle to the teaching/learning experiences as appropriate for each youth. I am elated that community educators reported that this same principle undergirds their practices in the development of youth and is reflected in the outcomes young people achieve.

As you read and the stories unfold, the belief in this principle is constantly revealed. Notice what possibilities for your community, if any, emerge. Neither this book nor belief in this principle is a tool, technique, or "silver bullet." I wonder whether this unintended discovery of agreement is a game changer that can inspire collaboration and relationship building among citizens and educators that expands our thinking of "who educates" and achieves the greatest benefit for our entire population of young people.

You decide . . .

With deep respect,
Patricia Moore Harbour

CHAPTER ONE

EDUCATION—
NOT JUST
SCHOOLING

Education is the deliberate, systemic, and sustained effort to transmit, evoke, or acquire knowledge, values, attitudes, skills, and sensibilities, as well as any learning that results from that effort, direct or indirect, intended or unintended.

Lawrence Cremin, American Education: The Metropolitan Experience

Throughout my adult life, education has been at the heart of my work. As a teacher, administrator, teacher trainer, researcher, and consultant, what has compelled my passion is a burning desire and commitment to ensuring that all human beings, especially young people, have the opportunity to be all they can be. I have long been dedicated to the creation of environments and experiences that are accepting and supportive and that foster the kind of confidence and belief in self that enables us to bring the best of who we are to our own lives and the lives of others.

This book documents the Kettering Foundation (KF) community educators research conducted between 2007-2010. The work of the citizens described in this book illustrates some of the ways that communities are educating young people to become the next generation of confident, competent, contributing citizens.

Education and Democracy

The community educators research was designed to examine several questions: Who are the community educators? What do they do? What motivates them? Underpinning these questions—and all of the Kettering Foundation's research—is a single question: what does it take to make democracy work as it should? The community educators research, therefore, explores its three questions through the lens of the relationship between education, community, and democracy, and asks, more specifically, what is the public's role in and responsibility for education in a democracy?

This set of questions establishes the contextual framework for this book. Furthermore, stories from my own experience in public education and the research of leaders in education and community development help to illustrate how the public's engagement and strategies for improving education have evolved over time. Such a framework lays the foundation from which you, the reader, are invited to consider what we learned through the course of our research.

The community educators study was implemented through a series of research conversations that included members of social and civic organizations, youth advocates, social-service practitioners, youth-development professionals, and leaders of various youth-oriented programs. All of the participants worked either directly with young people or were involved with the operations of programs engaged in some aspect of youth development. They represented, for example, small programs founded by private individuals, local chapters of large public and private organizations, community-based social and civic organizations, nonprofit institutions, and government agencies.

Whether intended or not, such youth-development organizations are reengaging the public and broadening the definition of education. This youth-development movement seems to operate on the belief that comprehensive education for young people expands beyond schooling, academic skills, facts, and standardized-test performance. In this broader view, the public must be involved in the education and development of youth; in a democratic society, the public has both a role in, and a responsibility for, education.

Education and democracy are fundamentally connected, with education a crucial thread in the fabric of the democratic process. This relationship between education and democracy is the subject of much of the work of philosopher and educator John Dewey. One of the foremost thinkers of the 19th and 20th centuries, Dewey is credited with launching the movement for experiential learning. Inspired directly or indirectly by Dewey, youth-development programs represented in the community educators study are engaging young people in all manner of experiential learning.

In Suffolk, Virginia, for example, I visited the Youth Public Safety Academy and witnessed young people learning how criminal investigators gather information to identify suspects. My excitement matched that of the teenagers' when one of them explained, "This is like they do on CSI," as he made a mold of a footprint and "read" the clues the footprint revealed.

John Dewey believed that in a democracy, education can enable the citizen to integrate culture and vocation. His theory is evident in what he perceived to be the role and responsibility of schools, describing them as both a social center and a place for instruction. Dewey believed that, in a democracy, there is a fundamental connection between social action and education; he saw a role for schools and citizens that affirmed a bond between education and the democratic process. Dewey ascribed to the schools the job of teaching young people both how to be effective problem solvers *and* how to live in a democracy.

This relationship between education and democracy provides a powerful lens through which to consider the relationship between the public's and the school's roles and responsibilities in education. In the early years of this country, education had a distinct connection with the institutions of the community. Schooling was primarily the responsibility of parents and the family, and additionally, learning occurred in the general activities of community life. In some communities, school was conducted in churches and other public places. In many others, the one-room schoolhouse was the center of the community, and often community and social activities were held in these schools.

For many years, school buildings were also the site for communities to deliberate and resolve civic issues, including issues about public education itself. School buildings were used as voting places, a democratic practice that continues today in a great many public school locations.

Over time, however, schools became more disconnected from their communities, and the bond between education and democracy suffered. And, as schools became more and more isolated from their communities, they began to be perceived more and more often as the only source of education.

That bond between the community and its public schools is crucial to ensuring that a democracy works as it should locally, both now and in the future. Citizens learn together how to identify and name the problems that affect their communities, as well as the quality and conditions of their individual and collective lives. In a democracy, citizens engage in civic deliberation and resolve problems for the benefit and well-being of their community, the citizenry, and future generations.

Education strengthens civic engagement and citizen participation for self-rule, voting, organizing, and reform. Citizens, learning together, deepen understanding among individuals and groups of citizens beyond their different perspectives and ideologies. Positive and diverse working relationships that build a viable community are among the advantages of a community's conscious awareness of the relationship between education and democracy.

This essential relationship is constantly being tested in countries around the globe and in the United States. In some of the most notable examples, countless citizens stood up to dictators, risking their lives for freedom, as the Arab Spring swept across the Middle East in 2011. Rejecting the kind of feeble "reform" their leaders offered, these citizens demanded the transformation that would fundamentally reinvent their countries and their lives.

With a new level of individual and collective awareness, and a shift in the citizens' hearts and minds, that kind of change is possible. Yet some people do not change until, as American civil rights leader Fannie Lou Hamer would say, "They are sick and tired of being sick and tired of the way that it is."

In many US communities, parents and other adults say they feel blocked from contributing meaningfully to schools. I wonder whether community educators, in spite of—or perhaps because of—that inability to contribute, are stepping up to rediscover the public's role in the development and education of youth. Are they "sick and tired of being sick and tired" of the way it is, of struggling to make a contribution?

Who Were the Educators in the Community?

When I was a child, it seemed that everybody in the community—neighbors, family and friends, churches, businesses, social and civic organizations—was somehow involved in our development. Everyone seemed to have an interest and a stake in the education and development of youth.

The title of Hillary Clinton's 1996 book *It Takes a Village* reportedly comes from an old African proverb. "It takes a village to raise a child" might be interpreted, in part, as a call for putting the public back into public education. The book has been challenged and criticized by some, and yet it has struck a chord with many other Americans. Conversations among my friends and colleagues often begin, "Back in the day . . .," and go on to recall a time when adults in the neighborhood along the path between home and school informally monitored young people as they traveled back and forth. These neighbors congratulated children on their successes, and they disciplined and warned them: "I will call your mama if you don't straighten up." They also mentored, guided, listened, and taught the community's young people countless life lessons.

As I prepared this book, I found myself reflecting on the south-west Virginia community of Roanoke, where I grew up. I thought about my experiences as a young person there, and about how the community impacted me and other young people at the time. My "village" included many Roanokers—my mother and father, my grandmother and grandfather, neighbors, members of social and civic organizations, teachers, my peers and their older siblings, college students and recent graduates, and local business owners. My schools and the church community played a huge role, not just in academics, but in political and civic learning, ethics, and life skills. More people than I could possibly mention contributed to my young life and development. Perhaps most important, the people of my community taught me to believe in myself. They were nurturing, and they cultivated trusting, caring relationships. They held high expectations for me, beginning when I was very young. Neighbors, family, friends, local leaders—both black and white in this segregated community—inspired me to lead and to achieve.

In my community I had opportunities to use my talents and to actively engage in social, civic, and political activities. I remember being a panelist and speaker for the local "diverse teen forum on race," to promote cross-cultural understanding among teenagers. I was a speaker in the local "I Speak for Democracy" competition. I was a summer youth teacher in the arts and drama for elementary-aged children at the YWCA. These experiences were available to me because of the efforts of local residents who provided time, attention, and mentoring skills. These learning experiences, in addition to what my friends and I learned in school, contributed to our education and development.

Miss Inez Smith, Mrs. Sallye Coleman, and Mrs. Gertrude West, residents of my neighborhood and community, were among my many role models and mentors. They were also local educators. Mrs. Coleman was my seventh and eighth grade social studies teacher. Mrs. West was our Girl Scout leader as well as a supervisor in the school district. Miss Smith was a family friend living on the next street and an English teacher.

Miss Inez, who would later become Mrs. Hanley, inspired my love for reading and reciting poetry; she taught me the beautiful and powerful poetry of James Weldon Johnson and coached me to memorize and recite my favorite, "The Creation," for many different audiences. (Years later, I taught it to my youngest daughter, Wenda, who won a local high school competition for her dramatic presentation of the poem.) These early experiences were the foundation for my lifelong love of and success in public speaking.

Mrs. West was involved with her Girl Scouts beyond the work required for us to earn our merit badges. She challenged us to excel in academics. She helped us to develop self-confidence and to stand with dignity as we engaged in interracial activities, in a community where segregation existed in schools, neighborhoods, public places, and even churches of the same religious denominations. Mrs. West, through the Girl Scouts, was our mentor for civic learning and engagement.

In school, when Mrs. Coleman taught me and my two best friends, Antoinette and Edith, she made social studies come alive for us, by making the subject real and relevant to our lives. She was also our advocate and supporter, encouraging us to lead, to excel academically. After school, Mrs. Coleman and her husband, who was a school principal in the district, had us in their home on many occasions.

My favorite memory from those visits is the time when she taught us how to make potato salad. Later, in a home economics class, we asked our teacher, Mrs. Thomas, if we could prepare lunch to celebrate Mrs. Coleman's birthday. She agreed and helped us with the menu. Because Mrs. Coleman had taught us how to make potato salad, we included that in our menu—hoping to surprise her with how well we could make it. We were ready to bring Mrs. Coleman into the room for her surprise, when "someone" (me, I think) got the idea that the potato salad should be yellow. We did not know to use mustard, so we looked for yellow food coloring. There was no yellow food coloring. Determined to make the potato salad special and pretty, we used blue instead! This did not make our home economics teacher happy, but Mrs. Coleman ate it and loved it. I still prepare this dish for my family today—but without the food coloring!

In high school, upset when I received my first-ever C grade, I marched to the office to inform my principal that I wanted to drop chemistry. He talked with me and assured me I could excel in chemistry as I had in other science courses. Instead of either approving or denying my request, he offered to tutor me and said that if I still didn't understand or improve my grade, he would allow me to drop the course. I did not know at the time that Mr. Phillips had majored in chemistry in college, but I agreed to let him help me. He was right: I regained my confidence, learned the material, and improved my grade. There is no question his belief in me made a huge difference.

My community—my village—stood by me up to and beyond graduation from high school. I received several scholarships to college, and I was encouraged, supported, and expected to do well. I was lucky to have a loving and supportive family, as well as a village, to help me succeed and thrive.

As I reflected on these personal experiences in the light of the community educators research, I considered the connection between school and community. Teachers and administrators in my community's school district were actively and deeply engaged with youth, both in school and in after-school activities.

Yet "educators" were not the only ones involved in my education. I remember many after-school experiences, some structured, some informal. Mr. Beamer, an entrepreneur and the owner of a local ice cream parlor, encouraged me to do well in school, offering ice cream cones as rewards for my successes. He also talked to me about the ice cream and showed me how to dip it; he showed me how to work the cash register and serve customers—even though I was too young to do much and I could not reach over the top of the counter. Yet by showing that he cared, he nurtured my growth and development. I was inspired by his entrepreneurial spirit.

Peer learning was also important in my village. Connie Terrell, a teenager who lived down the street, taught me to ride her bicycle when I was five years old. When my bicycle came, I already knew how to ride.

Our village placed a high value on educating youth, and belief in that value was widespread. That belief also went beyond a narrow definition of "education," to include a focus on developing youth to become "good people." I have always aspired to make my community proud. I hope in some way, I have.

Many of us who grew up in villages like mine have stories to tell about such formal and informal programs, both inside and outside school. Even those of us with vastly different backgrounds and life experiences can identify with each other as we share memories of the adults who made a difference in our lives. For instance, my friend and colleague Phil Stewart told me about the citizens in his community who supported his growth and development. Phil, a white American growing up in mid-20th-century New England, had little in common with me, an African American girl growing up a few years later in a segregated Southern city, but both Phil and I had loving families and other adults in the community who contributed to making us who we are today.

Warm memories flooded Phil's face as he told his story about Camp Berwick and how he came to be there for the first time in the late 1940s:

> My introduction to Berwick began with a phone call from one of my paper route customers, Mrs. Oliver Stone, whose husband was a well-respected local judge. She told me that she had recommended me to a summer camp on an island in Maine called Camp Berwick, run by a Dr. Berry, and asked if that would interest me. I was now 14, soon to be 15, and anxious to become an adult, and frankly, to get away from a loving but chaotic and stifling home life. So I immediately said I was interested, but neither I nor my parents had any money to pay for such a luxury. Mrs. Stone indicated that

the participation fee was minor, and said that she would handle it, as she felt I had "a lot of promise."

After a fitful night of trying to sleep in a crowded car, we arrived at the crest of a modest hill with grassy fields spreading out on both sides of the road. I saw Dr. Berry, who everyone simply called "Doc." I had met him once, several years earlier, when he had stitched a serious cut on my hand. I recognized him now by his broad, warm, welcoming smile, the way he peered directly into each boy's eyes, making each feel special and important to him. On that summer afternoon at Camp Berwick, Doc explained that the group had a simple task: in the next four or five days, we were to plant 10,000 balsam fir seedlings, which, when fully grown in 7 or 8 years, would provide us with Christmas trees, whose sale would help to support the camp. Doc showed us how to plant, how to take a spade and push hard enough on it with your foot to cut through the thick grass. I'd never done work like this in my life.

An 18- or 19-year-old third-year veteran was in charge of us three new boys, but things did not go as quickly as planned. When we still had six or seven thousand seedlings to plant, I began to get really tired, so to speed things up just a bit, I began planting two, then three, then a whole bunch of seedlings per hole. Of course, Doc eventually found out about this, and he let me know that it was unacceptable. In fact, Doc never hesitated with directness and firmness respecting any transgressions—or with praise for a job well done.

So, what was it that turned a young boy who had never experienced intense and very difficult physical labor, such as on that April trip, into an enthusiastic Berwick Boy for life? There is no simple explanation. As I reflect back, it is almost like a kaleidoscope, consisting of many parts whose relationships change with time. The first of those parts was Doc's magnetic personality. You could not help but feel larger, safer, more grown-up in his presence. Explaining his own tireless efforts at and on behalf of the camp, Doc would often say, "There is no greater pleasure than working very hard at something you love." I've never met another person in my life who so fully, almost magically, inspired me—as he did with nearly everyone who encountered him—to strive with all of my energy, intelligence, and drive (most of which I hadn't previously known that I possessed) to achieve the goals he set and the ambitions he unleashed in me.

The older boys at camp added another important dimension to the experience. Before then, I hadn't played any team sports, nor had any other experiences with groups of boys. When we younger boys at camp did our part, the older boys made us feel accepted, part of the group. This felt good. Working and "suffering" through the week with the other first-year boys developed a camaraderie among us that was not only novel for me, but very pleasant. Mixed in with all of this was the slowly dawning realization that hard work could indeed be fun. It made me feel good all over, even when I was bone tired. I could not but feel, having accomplished all that we did during those 10 days, that I was no longer just a boy; I was becoming a man. Doc's treating each of us like men, showing genuine respect for a job well-done, encouraged and constantly reinforced those feelings. I never would have believed I/we could accomplish so much. That first week at Camp Berwick encouraged me, for the first time in my life, to know that I could accomplish things I never would have believed possible before.

My experiences as a youth in Roanoke, and Phil's memories of Camp Berwick, make it clear that the concept we call "community educators" is not new. I am amazed at how similar our youthful experiences were, given that we lived in different parts of the country and our backgrounds and lifestyles were so different. Yet the outcome of our experiences with community members had much in common: both of us, looking back, are still filled with gratitude for the difference that these special people made in our lives. Phil left his camp experience every year inspired by his encounters with Dr. Berry and pleased with his progress as he matured into a man. My teachers and other members of the Roanoke community filled me with confidence and the belief that I could do anything I wanted in life, if I truly put my mind to it.

As adults, both Phil and I have engaged with young people in ways similar to how our elders had encouraged and motivated us. Phil continues to return to Camp Berwick to spend six weeks with the young men who attend each summer. In the 1970s, while I was working as a third-grade teacher, I founded and directed the Village Players, an after-school and weekend improvisational theater for children and young people in Reston, Virginia.

Thinking of that group, I am reminded of one of my third-grade students, Nan Rich, an avid reader who always had her nose in a book. Although her mother was pleased that her daughter liked to read, at the same time, she wanted her to develop more social and communication skills. Nan, the middle child between an older sister and a younger set of twin girls, was quite shy. Her mother thought it might help for her to participate in the improvisational theater. She was right; the experience was transforming for Nan. She quickly grew to love theater, and through the characters she developed, she found herself. Her mother was most pleased, exclaiming on one occasion, "Before, we were concerned that Nan would not talk, and now she has so much to say, we cannot get her to stop!" For me, seeing Nan develop was like watching a rosebud open into full bloom.

When I moved from Reston, I discontinued the Village Players Theater, but I have continued to work with young people as a mentor and role model. In every community where I have lived as an adult, I have tried to identify with one or two children and build a relationship with them, hoping to share what was given to me when I was their age. With these children, I have planned special days for us to spend together. On "Pat Harbour and Sara Bloom Day" in California, for example, my young friend Sara would visit my home, we would go and do something fun together, and then, before returning her to her parents, we would go out and have a Chinese dinner. We had long talks about her interests and curiosities. Another young friend, Daniel, was interested in other countries, so whenever I traveled to another country, I would bring him back something he requested that was peculiar to the history of that country. Leah, Bianca, and I toured the zoo together and were mutually frightened by the snakes, but we all enjoyed the train ride through the zoo.

These relationships have been exceedingly rewarding for me, and I often feel I learned as much from these young people as they imagine they learned from me. I am still in touch with many of them, and with their parents. Tara is another special friend of mine, whom I've known since she was born; she and I still talk on a regular basis—having long ago "adopted" each other as god-mother and goddaughter.

Reflecting on these stories, both about my own youth and about my adult experiences with young people, I am reminded of the role a community can play in developing youth to be good students and good citizens. I am also reminded of the powerful, positive difference a one-to-one, quality experience with an adult can make in a young person's life.

Is there a person who had a special meaning for you in your youth, and whom you have not forgotten to this day? If so, take a moment now and remember that person. Who was it? What kind of experiences did you share? How did those experiences make you feel? What influence, if any, has this person or the experiences you shared had since that time?

Reform or Transformation?

Hillary Clinton's *It Takes a Village* is much more than a reminder of what it was like in "the good old days" of my youth and the youth of my friend Phil. Rather, I see it as a call to citizens to participate in a transformation of education, by engaging the talents and gifts of the community as powerful resources for the development and education of youth. Is this the kind of transformation that today's community educators are helping to bring about?

To effect transformation, or systemic change, people in a community must examine their thinking about traditions, belief systems, differences, political ideologies, social behaviors, and relationships among all sectors in the community, including schools, and the bond between education and community. Most important, the community must be an integral part of any transformation of education. Without collective involvement, schools might achieve *reform*, but not the kind of lasting, stable transformation that leads to long-term positive impact on young people and the communities they live in.

Of course reform is easier than transformation. In reform we see modifications of a little of this and a little of that, improving, but not necessarily changing, the education system. We know we cannot create a different result with the same structure and elements.

Reform reminds me of my daughters, Lisa and Wenda. In each of their homes, I have rarely seen the furniture arranged the same way twice. Both frequently move their furniture, changing the dining room to the living room or the living room to the family room. Lisa regularly changes the color scheme throughout her house, and I have even walked in to find no walls where, the last time I visited, there were walls. My daughters' changes enhanced the aesthetics of the areas they modified. They improved the attractiveness of their homes, the flow of traffic between rooms, the comfort of the living area. Their new arrangements are always beautiful, and yet, they do not change the basic structure of the house.

Reforming schools is certainly of more consequence than redecorating one's home. Yet it appears that educators, including me, often focus on "reforming" selected aspects of schooling, with results that may improve one particular area, but that do not change education as a whole system.

As an educator working in school districts in Virginia; Washington, DC; and Ohio; or consulting in places like New York, California, and Louisiana, I have observed and trained educators, and I have taken leadership roles in a variety of reform efforts. Common among educators in these districts was our belief that we were transforming education, when in truth our work was merely "reforming" it. In the end, we merely changed one or two dimensions of schooling.

Some of these reforms included teaching math in new ways, integrating reading or writing into all curriculum areas, connecting businesses with schools, and moving from self-contained classes to family or multi-age groupings. Changes in pedagogy, curricula, and teaching methods reigned as frequent reform strategies in school districts across the country, as did changes in the amount of time students spent on tasks, the length of the school day or school year, and experiments in regrouping the grade levels that comprised an elementary, middle, junior high, or high school. None of these efforts, however, amounted to systemic change; rather, even when they were successful, all of these efforts led simply to improvements in selected parts of schooling or the school system.

Through my years in public education, I had the opportunity to view reform strategies from many different positions. In retrospect, I can see that in every case, we defined education narrowly, as "schooling." We certainly believed in involving parents and community, and in some ways we believed we were doing just that. For example, when I was a principal in Fairfax County, Virginia, we included large numbers of parent volunteers in school activities. In the 1980s, I worked with the superintendent in the District of Columbia Public Schools. In her Public-Private Partnership program, Floretta McKenzie engaged business executives and leaders to work with several high school magnet programs to ensure that graduates met the necessary academic requirements to enter college and gain work experience in the career area that the particular program emphasized. Members of the business community developed curricula and provided paid internships for these high school students and externships for their teachers. And in the public schools of Cleveland, Ohio, where I was an administrator in the 1990s, parents and a few members of the broader community participated in a series of meetings that resulted in shared decision making for the local schools. In the following passages, I offer more detailed description of those reform efforts, each of which resulted in some success—and some disappointment.

A View of School Reform from the Inside

In Virginia's Fairfax County Public Schools in the late 1960s and early 1970s, reform was a districtwide effort to ensure that the classroom environment and the school's organization fostered and supported a student-centered environment and individualized instruction, and focused on the development of the whole child. To prepare every school in the district to participate, 4 three-member resource teams served as staff-development trainers for the schools in each of the four regions of this 10th largest and highly respected school district. While I was a classroom teacher in the district, I was invited to be a trainer on one of those teams.

Prior to this assignment we, resource team members, were prepared for our role as trainers at a special summer-school session—a training lab in partnership with the School of Education at the University of Massachusetts. Professors and doctoral students from the university worked with us in an experiential "train the trainer" program, teaching us techniques and strategies for improving the quality of teaching and ensuring student achievement.

In morning sessions during the summer of 1970, students from across the district—students of all ability levels and from all demographic groups—learned in classrooms through innovative teaching strategies, and a school organization structure that was led by the university team. As the students learned, we also learned, by doing. When the students went home, we spent the rest of the day learning still more, through staff-development sessions, analysis, and assessments of the teaching and learning activities. This process increased our growth and development—and love for the work.

An essential aspect of our training was a method of clinical supervision introduced by the distinguished educator Robert Goldhammer, who based his model on the supervisory and evaluation methods used in teaching hospitals to perfect the specialized knowledge and skills of medical practitioners. The relationship between evaluator and teacher was a key component of Goldhammer's process, which was used in Fairfax County because it offered the possibility for purposeful evaluation, higher accountability, and enhancement of the teachers' professional development. At the conclusion of this summer program, not only were we better prepared for students in our respective schools, but we also left more competent and passionate about teaching.

In the fall of that same year, 1970, Beverly Mattox, Irene Lober, and later, Margo Koryda, and I became the district's Area III region's staff-development team. We worked with 40 schools providing staff development for teachers and principals. The primary focus of this reform effort was the innovations and strategies designed to ensure that both the teaching-learning process—and the way in which the school was organized—were child-centered.

In each school in Area III, my teammates and I conducted an intense, two-week teaching-learning laboratory filled with experiential practice, demonstration teaching, clinical supervision, and training workshops. In one-on-one sessions, we coached and facilitated principals in organizational development, clinical supervision, and ways to engage parents in the teaching-learning process. Even though several administrators resisted the changes, overall, these efforts to create local school change were very promising.

In hindsight, however, I recognize two stumbling blocks that may have limited our chances for long-term success: first, although we were from the Fairfax district, the resource team members did not come from the individual local schools. Second, I don't recall any action when schools, principals, or staffs involved informed the broader community, particularly the community beyond parents. This probably inhibited a sense of local ownership and responsibility for the outcome. Unintentionally, our team may have been perceived by some local school principals and their faculties as the "experts coming to change them."

Ultimately, as I recall, several principals decided not to offer the innovative training program to their school staffs. Others agreed at first, but after our two weeks on site, several returned the operation of their schools to the way they had been before. One teacher told us that the day we left the building, the principal called a meeting to tell his faculty bluntly, "We're not making any of those changes."

Still, a number of schools welcomed the innovations, but even they failed to adequately involve parents and other "outsiders" until after the changes were made. We as trainers acknowledged the need to engage parents and encouraged school principals to inform them of the changes to come and to explain how the innovations would benefit their children. I believe the team failed to emphasize the importance of this, since a training module that focused on engaging parents and community was not included. However, in nearly all the schools that implemented the dramatic changes, parents were simply informed after the fact.

In some school communities, parents accepted the change; in other schools, parents objected. I am still unsure whether the objection was to the change per se, or whether the opposition arose because parents had no voice in planning for it.

Two years later, I became principal of Timber Lane Elementary School, one of the schools where my resource team and I had spent two weeks training the faculty and staff in the innovative reform methods. To meet reform goals when I became principal, we created a student-centered environment, reorganized the school from self-contained classes to multi-aged groupings, and introduced team-teaching to the classrooms. Selected master classroom teachers became "Team Leaders," who supported three to four other teachers on their team. Our classroom teaching embraced accountability to strengthen student progress. Teachers generated educational plans for all students, not just for those with learning challenges.

Through these efforts, we aimed to improve student reading ability schoolwide. We also intended to increase the number of parent volunteers in the school. To help us reach these goals, we applied for and received a two-year grant of $50,000 per year, from the Office of Education, a part of the federal Department of Health, Education, and Welfare, as part of the national "Right to Read" effort. Our grant's title, "I Believe I Can Read," emphasized the relationship between a child's learning, self-confidence, and self-esteem. Within two or three years, our students' reading levels improved across the board—exponentially for some. Team leaders received a stipend for their administrative and staff-development role.

Also during this period, parent involvement in the school increased from less than 10 to nearly 100 volunteers. We organized in teams, with teachers holding leadership and management responsibilities for each team. Students were given more time for learning tasks, and instruction was offered in larger blocks of time for stu-

dents to learn at their own pace. Everyone in the school—
including the janitor, the principal, secretaries, kitchen staff, and
parent volunteers—was engaged in educating the students when
it was appropriate. Students with learning challenges were main-
streamed with some classes to better meet their educational and
social needs.

Our students made significant progress, and the school was
recognized and commended by school board members, local newspapers, congressional representatives who visited our campus, and
numerous educators in other school districts. The *Washington Post*
published glowing reports of our accomplishments. Still, some
parents strongly objected to the innovations and changes in the
organization of the school.

When I was hired as principal of Timber Lane, the Area Superintendent asked me to reform the school, whose principal was
retiring and where countywide innovations and reform practices had
not been implemented. I took my assignment to heart. The two weeks
I spent there the previous two years served as an excellent source of
diagnostic information to identify reform strategies appropriate for
the school. It is important to note that we were improving the school
rather than transforming education. Just as it had been through the
school district, the broader community and parents were informed
about the changes, rather than engaged in discussion prior to
implementation.

By the mid-1970s and through the early 1980s, many parents
across the nation, including Virginia, were involved in a "back-to-
basics" movement that was gaining popularity and resulted in re-
versing changes for many schools. Several other districts and schools
had implemented the same kinds of reforms we had implemented at
Timber Lane, and in many cases, those reforms were reversed. Walls
went up where they had been taken down; innovations like team
teaching and the use of learning centers and block scheduling were
ended; teachers went back to lecturing in front of the class. I wonder whether it would have been different at Timber Lane, if we had
engaged parents and the larger community in the planning.

We, the educators, missed an opportunity to learn about the community's values and to find out what parents wanted for their children. Parents may have received the information we wanted them to understand and accept, but their voices had not been heard.

Members of the larger community were only tangentially involved with the school, through, for example, student field trips to local sites, students spending the day with their parents in the workplace, and business leaders or other community members sharing their work and travel experiences in the classroom. Unlike the programs I would later learn about through the Kettering Foundation's community educators research, Timber Lane's after-school extended daycare program was a help to parents, but it offered little more than babysitting services and recreational activities. Nevertheless, the Timber Lane project led to positive results: the entire school staff worked together to create a supportive environment for our students; students themselves increasingly took pride in their school; incidents of vandalism stopped completely; and academic achievement and progress increased.

I was proud of what we achieved at Timber Lane and was happy to serve there as principal, but after just a few years, I received a national award that was difficult to refuse. In 1975, I accepted 1 of just 10 fellowships offered that year in the US Department of Health, Education, and Welfare, where I would have the opportunity to work with the HEW Secretary. Two years later I became a Special Assistant to the Commissioner of the Office of Education, and where I was involved with programs and policies that impacted education from the federal level.

I was recognized as a competent leader at Timber Lane, and, as numerous education researchers have reported, instructional leaders are critical to effective schools and school districts. However, again the focus was on reform, on improving the school. The staff did a great job with that. And yet, reform was not enough to sustain the change and gains made. I had not adequately engaged the parents and community at a level where they had ownership for the education of their young people. We wanted the same things, but we were working along parallel paths with two different agendas that did not connect. As professional educators, like so many others, we worked in isolation.

The corollary to the assertion that instructional leaders are important to effective schools is that changes in leadership can be disruptive or a barrier to educational transformation, particularly when new leadership often means the discontinuation of improvements that have shown positive results. When I left Timber Lane, the new principal's ideas about structuring, the learning environment, and the roles and organization of teachers, were the exact opposite of mine. So the school returned to its former organizational and teaching-learning practices.

Only later did I learn of the extent to which things had changed. Before I left Timber Lane for my HEW fellowship, the National Education Association (NEA) approached me about writing an article for one of their publications, to share with other educators some of the innovations we had tried and the progress we were making. I invited our reading program coordinator, Linda Goldberg, to write the article, which was accepted with enthusiasm. But the publication was delayed. Two years later, when both Linda and I were no longer at Timber Lane, an NEA staff member called the school, asking to photograph some students to accompany the article. Confused by the school's response, the magazine's editor called me at home one evening. I informed her that I was no longer the principal at Timber Lane and suggested that she contact the school directly. To my surprise, she responded, "I did—and they told me, 'We no longer teach reading here.'"

Well, so much for school reform!

Perhaps we had the right intentions, but in the end, our school reforms amounted to moving the furniture around, rather than systemically transforming the whole. We neglected to engage parents and community members in sharing ownership for education in the Timber Lane community. And, although leadership is a key ingredient to successful reforms, a change in leadership would not have mattered so much if another key ingredient—community ownership—had been in place to serve as a counterbalance. A new principal could not reasonably have considered overturning reforms if parents and community had been genuinely engaged in and committed to those reforms.

In the 1980s, I was involved with another kind of school-reform effort in Washington, DC, a Public-Private Partnership, or PPP. These innovative programs were an outgrowth of the Adopt-a-School movement, which we will examine further in the following chapter.

In Washington, then-superintendent Floretta McKenzie, a well-known urban school leader and innovator, launched a Public-Private Partnership to better prepare young people for college and a career. At their core, these partnerships focused on specialized academic curricula, practical work experiences for students, and teacher externships. Housed in five high schools across the school district, the rigorous in-school magnet programs were based on research that identified certain careers with the greatest potential for future employment opportunities. As with the Adopt-a-School effort, each PPP academic program had a corporate sponsor; unlike the Adopt-a-School programs, PPPs were based on a well-developed curriculum in a specific field of study with expected job growth.

In partnership with the schools and businesses, the initial five Public-Private Partnerships focused on careers in health professions, communications, business and finance, pre-engineering, and hotel management and culinary arts. Later, an international studies and an International Baccalaureate program were added. PPP students received paid summer internships in their field of study. In the hospitality program, for example, student interns were paid by the hotels and restaurants in which they worked; similarly, those studying business and finance were employed in and paid by local banks. Other students, with the support of Mayor Marion Barry, were paid through the Mayor's Summer Youth Employment Program.

McKenzie's vision advanced business partnerships to a new level, as she generated a different dynamic in the relationship between businesses and schools. Together, the two partners became cocreators, sharing responsibility for educating the high school students served by these programs.

A local school coordinator who was also an experienced teacher managed and implemented each PPP program. The role of the corporate partner was unique, as McKenzie invited local and national businesses to "roll up their sleeves and work" with teachers and program staff, to help create a difference in the learning experiences and curricula and to better prepare students for college and employment. She encouraged businesses to share ownership and responsibility for the education of these students, all the way to graduation—and beyond.

To initiate the effort, McKenzie requested a "loan executive," Lois Rice, from a major multinational company, who worked with the district superintendent and original PPP program staff to design the first PPP programs. The initial program was launched through Rice's efforts, and each partnership established a local school working committee that included teachers, staff, administrators, and representatives from corporations and small businesses working in the particular field the PPP program offered. This local working committee provided oversight for the program's curriculum, special classes, and progress. When Lois Rice's term as loan executive was over, McKenzie offered me the job of executive director, to oversee development and provide leadership for the collective partnership program and to create new PPPs. With enthusiasm, I accepted the position.

Again, I started a new journey in an urban school district focused on reform. During my tenure with the program, the relationship with the business community deepened, and their commitment to the program heightened. I organized a steering committee comprised of CEOs and high-ranking decision makers, to provide oversight and guidance for the overall mission of the Public-Private Partnership. At the local level, members of the corporate working committee taught classes and worked with staff to design and develop the curricula. The steering committee met regularly with the superintendent, the PPP executive director, and the local program directors. This committee provided the overall strategy for the success of the program and facilitated assignments of students and teachers for summer work and learning experiences. Corporate partners supported many graduates, enabling them to continue their education at leading universities and colleges, often the corporate executives' own alma maters. Students also returned to summer jobs during vacation prior to the fall semester. The PPP steering committee sponsored an annual recognition and awards program for graduating high school students. This event became a must-attend celebration in the community, and participants included students and parents, school board and city council members, the mayor, and community and business leaders.

The Washington, DC, Public-Private Partnership produced impressive, positive results for many high school students and changed the relationship between the business community and the district schools. The business community's involvement grew from disengagement to participation in a collaborative enterprise that cultivated shared leadership, responsibility, and ownership. At the same time, students were encouraged to advance their academic development, and the program produced graduates who were ready for the workplace and college.

These results, to a limited extent, comprehensively engaged a segment of the community; specifically, the business community took an active role in educating young people. However, other segments of the community clearly were not at the table. So in the end, this was a *reform* strategy that created change in a limited dimension of the school system, rather than a *transformation* of education. As discussed earlier in this chapter, there is an important distinction between reform and transformation. Education *reform* makes modifications to improve different segments of a school; to *transform* education means to change systemically all of its various dimensions, including its relationship with parents and the wider community, its curriculum and how it is delivered, expectations for student achievement, and its entire approach to teacher training.

I can offer yet another example of education reform, from my experience with public schools in Cleveland, where I served as chief-of-staff to the Superintendent of Schools in the early to mid 1990s, and later as assistant superintendent for 100 elementary schools. In our reform plan, "Vision 21," the district superintendent offered schools the opportunity to make regional and local decisions on the best reform methodology for their own schools. In each region, many groups of parents and other community members, teachers, and school staff met to discuss some of the research-based approaches to reform that had demonstrated successful outcomes in other school districts. These Vision 21 meetings were convened to answer the question, what do we really want our children to get from school? Participants deliberated over their different beliefs and values about education for the children in their community through public, deliberative forums similar to the National Issues Forums (NIF). Teachers, parents, community members, and administrators deliberated, over the course of several meetings, the issues central to *their* questions. This gave us an opportunity to understand where there was common ground. As a result, participants reached a collaborative decision and recommended to the superintendent which schools in each region would use which approach. When recommendations were forwarded to the district superintendent, Sammie Campbell-Parrish, at the completion of deliberations, she approved them without change. This process for engaging the public in education, unprecedented in this school district, accomplished the goals it set out to achieve.

Campbell-Parrish also offered a "co-op learning" approach, to ensure that parents had a voice in local school decision making; she intended for parents to be partners in the teaching-learning process in their children's schools. This approach, which had been very successful in private preschool programs, was an innovation that provided parents—the child's first teachers—the opportunity to participate meaningfully in the child's learning at school.

These efforts to involve parents were successful in many ways, but looking back, I see again that involving parents is not the same thing as engaging the broader community. To achieve sustainable, long-term transformation, the community must be meaningfully involved.

An unexpected consequence of the efforts to involve parents was that parents began to expect immediate, dramatic improvement—a quick fix. Parents and others, disappointed that schools were not doing better, became harsh critics of teachers, administrators, and teaching methods. As they demanded accountability, the media joined in, producing negative reports that were highly critical of every aspect of local schools. Newspapers in urban districts at the time usually had one or two reporters on the education "beat." In Cleveland, I remember two journalists whose articles almost always had a negative slant, denigrating some aspect of the local school district's staff, school board, or superintendent. Rarely do I recall reading any article under their by-line that celebrated the schools or the district. Following the rise of investigative reporting, it seemed they were fashioning themselves to be the second coming of Woodward and Bernstein, the *Washington Post*'s celebrated Watergate reporters.

Often it seemed their stories were looking for something that was not there or making something out of nothing. One day during lunch with one of these reporters, I dared to ask, "Does your newspaper in any way see its role as a corporate citizen with some responsibility for public education?" I added, "If I were a student, parent, or teacher in this community reading your coverage of my school system, I would be devastated and maybe come to loathe being a part of this school district." I received no real response to my concerns, and the negative focus of the articles did not change. The discontent in the community deepened and continued to grow.

The commonly held view that Cleveland's schools were "bad schools" continued to contribute to a lack of trust between the community and the schools, and a loss of public confidence in the schools. To make things worse, urban flight from public education often stripped public schools of diversity, as a majority of middle-class families of all ethnicities and backgrounds left for the suburbs.

Ultimately, much of the progress in engaging parents in the Cleveland schools was lost, as the district hired and lost a series of superintendents over a few years' time. Yet as with my experience in Fairfax County, perhaps a change in leadership would not have mattered so much had the broader community been more genuinely engaged.

All of these school districts benefitted to varying degrees from reform efforts that I was involved in, along with many other dedicated educators. In Fairfax County we initiated districtwide reforms to change the organizational structures for teaching and learning. In the District of Columbia, reforms were aimed at changing the relationship between schools and the business community. In Cleveland, we succeeded in bringing parents into the decision-making process. Yet in each case, those reforms failed to reach the level of transformation.

My experiences in public school systems, however, were not unusual. In the next chapter, we will take a look at other reform efforts in the context of some of the major research into educational theory and practice of the past century.

============ A STORY FROM THE FIELD ============

Life Experience as a Resource for Helping Youth

Mary K. Boyd

When I think of community educators, I think of two questions: who from the community does what to make a difference in the lives of youth? and who are the people who know best how to reach out and engage youth? Most of us know of the usual agencies, programs, and projects led by executives and implemented by youth workers. Such organizations are great for many of our youth, but they are not always able to "connect" with some of those most in need. Fortunately, there are certain grassroots community educators who, because of their own life experiences, are themselves the best resource for connecting with and helping to educate young people.

I know of two such people who walked some rough roads in life and came to rely on community resources to help them overcome many challenges; they in turn became resources for educating youth about how to navigate life's twists and turns. Dora founded and now directs a program called Mentoring Young Adults (MYA), and Kemet directs a youth drum and drill team called Flawless. Both programs have nonprofit 501(c)(3) status.

I met Dora when I was director of an alternative education program called Street Academy, cosponsored by the St. Paul Urban League, the University of Minnesota, and the St. Paul Public Schools (which was also the administrator). Street Academy served high school youth, ages 16 to 21, who felt disenfranchised by the traditional public school system. Dora was 14 and had nowhere else to go when she arrived there.

When Dora was in elementary school, she was transferred from a mostly black neighborhood school to which she could walk with friends, to a white elementary school outside of her community. Although well-intentioned, desegregation plans that bused African American students to predominantly white schools often were difficult for children, especially those from troubled families. As the second of five children born to two alcoholic parents, Dora was one such child, and the new school experience was somewhat traumatic for her. Even worse, she had had a close relationship with her father, which ended abruptly when she was 11 years old. Dora was at a gas station with her dad when he was violently killed, shot six times.

After her father's death, Dora's older sister ran away, and Dora looked for comfort and guidance in the youth centers near the projects where her family lived. Still, she was filled with unresolved emotions that even she did not understand. In junior high, her class watched *Roots*, the 1977 television miniseries about an American family descended from a West African Mandinka warrior who was kidnapped and sold into slavery as a teenager. Upset by the depiction of generations of African Americans being mistreated by whites, Dora said she would punch the first white person she saw . . . and she did just that. She punched a white girl and was administratively transferred to Street Academy. She was the youngest student we ever accepted.

At Street Academy Dora saw black teachers, black staff, and a black principal. This was a place that demonstrated community, and she felt accepted there. Although she was a challenge, we saw in her spirit, energy, drive, and lots of opinions. In addition to teaching her the academic subjects, we showed love, gave inspiration, and prepared her for re-entry into a traditional high school and community.

After she was at Street Academy for a couple of years, I encouraged Dora to attend Central High School because she needed to have that larger school experience with more options. We made sure we handed her off to key people on that staff who would continue to support and guide her toward graduation. They succeeded, and Dora was the first person in her family to graduate from high school.

After graduation, Dora completed an 18-month business school program. Nevertheless, between the ages of 18 and 25, she once again began to feel lost, thinking there was no one there for her as she transitioned from high school to the adult world. She used and sold drugs and got involved with the wrong men. Even though she remembered the influence of positive experiences at Street Academy, at the youth centers, and a few other places in the black community, Dora says she felt disconnected. She moved away from Minnesota for a few years, and then came back to St. Paul. Yet through all that time, she says, one thing she held onto was her love for her people.

As Dora grew older she began to recognize her need to "give back," and she came to realize that even if you touch just one child and make a difference in that child's life, that is giving back.

The turning point came in 2005, when Dora saw a young woman sitting on some steps with a bag of clothes and nowhere to live. She took the woman home and helped her to get a job and a place to live. That experience sparked something for Dora, and she decided to make it her mission to help young men and women to transition from youth to adulthood. Although she had never led any kind of organization before, Dora says she trusted in a Higher Power to guide and sustain the growth of her vision.

Although she worked informally at first, in 2008, Dora filed papers to officially found her organization, Mentoring Young Adults, whose mission is to help develop and empower young adults with self-esteem, motivation, and a vision for their lives. Its focus is on leadership development, employment, housing, secondary education, and entrepreneurial skills. MYA helps young adults, who in turn learn to help others. They learn about the political process by observing meetings of the city council and state legislature and by meeting in person with public officials. They tutor elementary students and help out in various ways around the community.

Dora believes in education as the basis and driving force for economic growth, workforce productivity, violence and crime reduction, and the building of strong families and strong communities for generations to come. She has found homes for the homeless and jobs for young people who need them; she constantly encourages continuing education. MYA members have conducted community forums about education and other important issues. Dora also serves as the "conscience" of the community, challenging the establishment when she thinks people are failing in their duties as citizens, failing to meet their responsibilities to one another.

Like Dora, Kemet found himself in an alternative high school program in St. Paul, after a number of difficult years in regular public schools—and a childhood and youth marked by hardship. Kemet was adopted by a great uncle and aunt when he was a baby, so he was raised by elders who were of an age more typical of grandparents. He recalls getting a lot of whippings as a child, but not much nurturing. His great aunt had been born on a plantation in Arkansas, so she herself must have had a hard life. She was, as he describes her, "old school." Kemet says he remembers always being very angry because, he believes, he did not have much of a childhood—no hugs or demonstrations of love, just custodial care. His great uncle passed away when Kemet was in the third grade, and the boy's life just got harder and poorer.

Kemet was gang-banging from the time he was 14 until he was 20. He lived in Oklahoma for about six months during those teen years and did the same things there. He came back to Minnesota and reunited with his mother in his late teens. His great aunt passed away, and six months later, so did Kemet's mother. It was just three years since he had reunited with her. Before she died, Kemet promised his mother that he would go back to high school and that he would graduate. Even though he had experienced many losses early in life and had been kicked out of several schools in St. Paul for fighting, he was determined to fulfill that promise. That is when I met him.

When he came to the Area Learning Center in St. Paul, Kemet was still deeply involved in gang culture. Yet he was shocked and pleased when I—a black female principal— challenged him, believed in him, accepted him, and was not afraid of him. The staff and I refused to tolerate his gang style of dress and lack of anger management, and ultimately he appreciated the high standards we set for him. He was very intelligent, wrote poetry, and joined the Half-Pintz community drum and drill team. He learned a lot about self-discipline from elders who saw his potential and took him under their wings.

Fulfilling the promise he made to his mother, Kemet graduated from high school. He also began to teach other young people how to channel their frustrations through drumming. He has been directing the Flawless drum and drill team for many years now, with female assistants who work more with the female youth on the drill team while he focuses on the drummers. Some 65 to 70 young people, ages 5 to 20, are in the organization at any one time. When asked about his method of engaging with the kids, Kemet says he "loves them as his own." He tries to keep it basic and simple, leading with an emphasis on discipline, focus, truth, and on having a "plan-full life" and a good education. Kemet says that when he was growing up, he hated his elders for not telling him the truth about life. That is why, he says, he lets the young people he works with know that life is tough and requires hard work and preparation. He gets his points across by telling them his own life story.

Kemet requires the youth in his program to give back and to stay connected to their community by doing community-service projects. He takes them to college campuses to encourage them to aspire to higher education. He exposes them to their history and helps them to build self-confidence through performance and by listening and talking to their elders.

Kemet strongly believes that you can feel when people really care about you. He recalls the time I took him to speak before the school board and the time I took him to appear on a program where he could share his poetry publicly before an audience. He continues to build on what he has learned by educating youth about life, opportunities, and responsibilities.

Every practice session for Flawless opens and closes with prayer. Kemet expresses the importance of spirituality as part of one's wholeness.

Kemet continues to avail himself of the teachings from community elders, some of whom are professional educators, teachers, and professors. He believes the youth can listen and learn from the stories the elders tell. He has embarked on closing the gap between the generations. One way he has done this is by holding open mic nights at Golden Thyme Coffee Shoppe, a popular gathering place in the local black community. The events provide an opportunity for elders to share their stories and for young people to ask questions and work toward an understanding of what life is all about.

Making a difference in the development and education of young people takes a variety of styles of engagement, including the grassroots, or "on-the-ground," efforts of community educators. Such caring people can be a powerful resource. I am very proud of Dora and Kemet and of their passion for making a difference in the lives of youth and the community.

Mary K. Boyd—is a retired St. Paul Public Schools administrator who, since retirement, has served in three interim positions, dean of the Hamline University Graduate School of Education, manager of the Department of Child Protection and Director of Services to Children and Families for Ramsey County in Minnesota. She is the president and CEO of MKB & Associates, Inc., a consulting organization that focuses on education and human services from a cultural perspective. She is very active in her community; serving on many boards and committees as well as mentoring and coaching youth in the schools on leadership development.

CHAPTER TWO

SCHOOL REFORM OR EDUCATION TRANSFORMATION?

Education is a lifelong process of which schooling is only a small but necessary part. The various stages of schooling reach terminal points. . . . But learning never reaches a terminal point.

Mortimer Adler, The Paideia Proposal

When I was a classroom teacher, we talked about change and about teaching "the whole child." Later, when I served as principal, instructional leader, and as assistant superintendent in various school districts, my colleagues and I were concerned with creating student-centered schools, revising curricula and instruction, improving teaching with new innovations, increasing parental involvement, and making numerous other improvements.

Such efforts were taking place in virtually every school in the nation, as teachers and administrators sought to keep up with changing expectations. Over the years, states implemented "competencies" and "standards" for learning, and eventually high-stakes tests came to determine who would graduate and who would not. National teacher examinations were ushered in, to ensure that qualified teachers were in the classrooms across the nation.

In states across the country, when school board members, the media, or parents have had concerns about one issue or another—falling math scores, high absenteeism, low graduation rates, for example—there's been a rush to fix, or reform, that problem. Rarely, however, was the issue examined in relationship to a whole system.

In the name of education reform, millions and millions of local, state, and federal dollars have been spent. Yet research suggests that school reforms, by and large, have not been sustained over time.

For decades, the professionals' efforts to change and reform education have focused on schooling and teachers, but this book also examines efforts to move the discussion to a broader view of education that goes beyond schools alone. Over the years, education has become synonymous with schooling, and in practice they have been generally considered as one and the same. In contrast, the community educators research examined the role of citizens and community resources in the development and education of young people. In these citizen-led programs, young people are being "educated" in ways that go beyond traditional academic measures, and in the process, they are expanding the definition of education beyond what schools alone can do.

Bob Cornett, a retired local government official, has been active for some time in after-school youth-development and education programs in his Kentucky community. During one community educators research conversation, he explained why he believes such programs are important: "I don't believe the schools are going to get 'fixed' until we fix the community." Community and schools, in other words, are one. Schools are an integral part of the community, and each is impacted by the level of effectiveness or ineffectiveness of the other. Schools are in the community, not an isolated, separate entity. It's not one or the other, but rather, "both, and."

With that thought in mind, I considered Bob Cornett's words: does he mean that in order to transform education, we must transform both the community and the schools in that community? And I reflected on all the reform efforts I'd been involved with over the years: in rural, urban, and suburban school districts, our efforts always focused on the schools alone. My colleagues and I had been smart enough to include the community—to an extent. The problem was that we had defined "community involvement" too narrowly, as minor participation from parents and businesses.

Trends in Education Research and Reform

Over the years, as reform of one kind or another has been implemented in most school districts across the country, some districts took a radical turn and privatized schools, using a business model as a strategy for reform. A number of school districts nationwide, for example, turned to Edison Schools, Inc., whose CEO, Christopher Whittle, proposed that through privatization, he could run "public" schools for less money than school districts could, and he could improve student achievement while also making a profit.

In recent years, interest in the business model and private management of schools as a means of reform seems to be declining, in comparison to the 1990s. Nevertheless, in more and more school districts, superintendents are using the title of "CEO," or Chief Education Officer. This trend, perhaps a remnant of the business model idea, may be an effort to acknowledge the professional status of school superintendents. There may be value in changing the mind-set, particularly of a local community, in order to recognize the superintendent's role and responsibility to be comparable to that of a corporate CEO, as a school district's CEO is both a business and education executive.

Market principles were also applied within and between school districts, through the "school choice" movement. Criteria like high scores on standardized and criterion-referenced testing were used to identify high- and low-performing schools, leading, naturally, to a greater demand among parents to enroll their children in schools with higher scores. Because of state funding formulas, public funds that had supported students in their previous, low-performing schools "followed" them to their new, high-performing schools— draining the resources available to serve the students who remained enrolled in the most troubled schools.

Additional trends in schools appeared in the 1980s and 1990s, as leading educators from prestigious universities conducted research that resulted in principles, practices, teaching-learning, and organizational strategies to reform and transform schools. School districts generally incorporated one plan or another. Following is a summary of some of the research that has influenced education reform in the United States.

In the late 1970s and early 1980s, Ron Edmonds—director, at that time, of Harvard's Center for Urban Studies—launched a movement that came to be known as the Effective Schools Movement. Edmonds collaborated with a cadre of educators, including Lawrence Lezotte, as well as other citizens and policymakers, to tackle school reform. School districts and educators across the country took an interest in the Effective Schools model.

Two profound beliefs were the foundation of Edmonds' work. First, he believed that schools can be changed and reformed to become effective for all students. He also believed that all children can learn and that we already know what is necessary to ensure that this becomes a reality. "We can," wrote Edmonds, "whenever and wherever we choose, successfully teach *all* children whose schooling is of interest to us. We already know more than we need to do that. Whether or not we do it must finally depend on how we feel about the fact that we haven't so far."

Edmonds and those with whom he collaborated based their

beliefs on research that identified several distinct characteristics of effective schools: instructional leadership, a clear and focused mission, a safe and orderly environment, high expectations, frequent monitoring of student progress, positive home-school relations, and adequate opportunity to learn and time on task.

Edmonds' research fueled an enthusiastic breakthrough among many educators and school districts. The Effective Schools Movement inspired a new mind-set for thinking about young people and their ability to learn. It also called forth changes in school culture and climate. This research-based process for school reform put the responsibility for basic skills, student achievement, and student progress in the hands of professional educators. At the same time, the role of parents involved in the education of their children was valued and recognized as highly important. Schools were called upon to be accountable.

The Effective Schools research demonstrated that all children can learn, regardless of family background, previous level of education, or economic status. The Effective Schools research refuted the earlier assumptions of James Coleman and other social scientists, who believed that children who came from poverty and unsupportive families could not learn, regardless of the instructional methodology used. The Effective Schools research clearly indicated not only that all children can learn, but that schools can make a difference for every child.

Howard Gardner's theories about multiple intelligences and different learning styles, first proposed in 1983, have also been among the most influential ideas applied to school reform in recent decades. These strategies focused on the different ways that students learn in order to facilitate a more successful teaching-learning process. For example, a child whose "artistic intelligence" is dominant may learn and understand the Lewis and Clarke expedition when the facts and history are presented through an art activity, rather than just through a written text.

Gardner, a professor of cognition and education at the Harvard Graduate School of Education, believes that as human beings, we have the intelligence through which we can learn how to gain knowledge, and to interact with and understand the world around us.

Ted Sizer, founder of the Coalition of Essential Schools (CES) in 1984, has been another leading educator and visionary for school reform. He established the Annenberg Institute for School Reform. Sizer's contribution is a philosophy and belief system for organizing schools. It is not a model for schools to replicate, but a way of thinking and a strategy for increasing academic achievement. Sizer believed that student achievement must be based on student competencies rather than the amount of content that is retained by the student. In Sizer's view, the role of the teacher changes from one who transmits knowledge, to a coach who supports students to take responsibility for their own learning. He is a staunch proponent of setting expectations for students that empowered them to do well because they were expected to do so. Sizer also identified parents as key collaborators of the school community.

The principles that emerged from the CES research describe the core beliefs and characteristics of Essential Schools: learning to use one's mind well; less is more; depth over coverage; goals apply to all students; personalization; student as worker and teacher as coach; demonstration of mastery; tone of decency and trust; commitment to the entire school; resources dedicated to teaching and learning; and democracy and equity.

In 2003, Sizer cofounded the Forum for Education and Democracy, a "national education 'action'" that is, according to its website, "committed to the public, democratic role of public education and the preparation of engaged and thoughtful democratic citizens."

James Comer, a child psychiatrist at Yale University, is known for the School Development Program, a school-reform approach that focuses on early childhood development. The program's primary purpose is to create a school and classroom environment where children feel "comfortable, valued, and secure." Comer believes this type of environment is an opportunity for children, parents, and school staff to develop a positive emotional bond and attitude toward the local school program.

Comer recognizes the importance of collaborative relationships among parents, teachers, students, the school, and service agencies in the community. In fact, health and social-service agencies are often housed in the schools, leading many educators to see the "Comer School" as a one-stop service center. This approach has been widely used with the intention of supporting children and their families by making services more accessible.

The School Development Program is often referred to as a reform strategy; however, Comer has said he believes that schools must be transformed. Comer understands that change must be systemic in order to make a sustainable difference. His process emphasizes the transformation of the school district, not just individual schools, including changes in the board of education, office of the superintendent, and local school. This transformation process includes policies and practices within the school system and collaborative relationships with service agencies in the community.

The research upon which the School Development Program is based was led by Comer and his colleagues at the Yale University Child Study Center. Over a two-year period, this study was conducted in two elementary schools in New Haven, Connecticut. According to the *Department of Education Consumer Guide*, Comer concluded "that children's experiences at home and in school deeply affect their psychosocial development, which in turn shapes their academic achievement. Conversely, poor academic performance is in large part a function of the failure to bridge the social and cultural gaps between home and school." In the community educators study, these are the gaps that programs seem to be emphasizing for youth—as will be discussed in later chapters of this book.

I have offered here a very cursory description of the enormous body of work of Edmonds, Gardner, Sizer, and Comer. All have written extensively, and their theories have had a profound impact on school reform over the past decades. Yet through the years, as schools incorporated these and other research-based methodologies or new trends into their reform efforts, citizens and parents have remained frustrated. As they sought opportunities to contribute to the education of young people, they often encountered a "we are the experts" attitude from education professionals, as well as bureaucratic red tape that was difficult, if not impossible, to break through.

Since the 1980s, schools and communities often have been at odds on matters regarding what should be taught and how it should be taught, as well as on matters of discipline and the measurement of academic achievement in schools. Teachers, parents, and administrators have blamed one another for failures in education. Businesses have accused schools of inadequately preparing graduates for the workplace, as some employers found themselves conducting basic skills training in reading, grammar, and writing for their employees. Each sector of the community expressed more and more frustration with schools.

Citizens' frustration over education worsened further, as a perception grew that schools were isolating themselves from the community. Parents increasingly felt as though they were "outsiders," who were not welcome on school grounds. It may be worth noting that some of the barriers arose from the increased attention paid to ensuring the safety of students, teachers, and administrators, in response to several high-profile instances of school violence. In any case, citizens were finding it more and more difficult to be a part of the education process. This fragmented relationship between schools and communities in effect barred the public from public education.

As a result, the sole responsibility for education seemed to be turned over to schools, so that when citizens convened to discuss *education*, the conversation all too often unraveled into emotionally heated and polarizing talk, narrowly focused on *schools*.

There always seems to be a new trend in education. The next one may have some benefits, but in the past, changing a few dimensions and dynamics of a school has not made a sustained difference in the big picture, education. Sustainable change does not require that particular strategies continue forever, but rather, that a school and its community continuously expand the thinking, relationships, and collaborative partnerships needed to develop and educate youth, the next generation of leaders. *Where communities are working toward this kind of change, as with some of the programs in the community educators study, are they creating a culture of learning that makes education everybody's business? Does this imply that citizens, not just professional educators, must be involved to transform education?*

I have noticed that reform efforts in many school districts have raised the bar by improving, for example, teaching methodologies, school governance, and teacher-training programs, but I have also noticed that many of these changes have been temporary. In far too many places, real modification has been limited, and authentic systemic change has been interrupted by competing forces, unable or unwilling to come together to establish and share ownership and responsibility for educating youth. This is evident in districts where school boards set aside important education decisions, to fulfill their own individual or political agendas.

Other impediments to progress that I've seen have included incompatible relationships between school boards and superintendents, which resulted in a change of superintendents, on average, every 18 months to 2 years. Relationships between parents and schools became more and more adversarial as bleak school rankings and test results created in the community a loss of faith in the local schools. In many urban settings, the inability of teachers' unions and the school district to find common ground seemed insurmountable.

It seemed as if over the years, with every step forward there have been 10 steps backward. Often through misunderstanding and a lack of communication, parents and the community did not comprehend what schools were doing and felt they no longer had access to those schools. They voiced their discontent in a number of ways, including the repeated defeat of school bond issues and an increase in home schooling and the creation of charter schools. Flight from public schools hastened, and in some cities, everybody who could, moved to the suburbs or enrolled their children in private or parochial schools. All of these factors created additional financial stress on public education.

In the 1970s and 1980s, these circumstances often resulted from the tensions created in the rousing "back-to-basics" movement. Like a snowball rolling downhill, the movement grew and spread across the country. In some districts, the push-back from schools produced even more isolation and separation from community.

During the height of this discontent, school administrators, teachers, and principals often resisted meaningful community engagement with the schools. Community members and parent volunteers were limited to activities like chaperoning field trips, baking cookies, working in the lunchroom, and keeping records for teachers.

Can Citizens Make a Difference?

Citizens across the country were frustrated and complained about the lack of access to "their" schools. Beginning in the 1970s and 1980s and continuing throughout the 1990s, many said they could not find a way to contribute or make a difference. Even now, more than a decade into the 21st century, we still find evidence of this problem.

Interestingly, some citizens in this period did find a way to contribute, although not in a way that gave them real entry to their schools. In 1978, the state of California passed Proposition 13, drastically reducing funding for its public schools. The S. H. Cowell Foundation, recognizing the fiscal peril of San Francisco's schools, provided a means for the private sector to generate resources to benefit teachers, students, and school sites. A citizen committee, led by executive director Gladys Thacher, worked with the district superintendent and the school board to build a bridge between the schools and the private sector. From this point, the formation of public education funds swept the country. These 501(c)(3) nonprofit organizations enabled parents and other citizens to provide additional funding beyond the school district's regular allocation to individual schools. In fact, one such public education fund raised more than $400,000 for one school in southern California. Although such situations raise concerns about inequities in school financing, because of the disparity among different communities' ability to contribute, public education funds became a frequently used vehicle for providing fiscal support to schools. Often support took the form of small grants made directly to teachers, or the purchase of equipment or services that benefited the school as a whole, individual classrooms, or a group of children within the student body. Citizens and parents could donate money yet they felt isolated and thwarted on how to make a meaningful difference in the education and development of youth.

Businesses Get Involved

Another kind of community involvement also began to surface in the late 1970s and early 1980s, as schools reached out to the business community to form partnerships, in which a local business "adopted" a particular school. The business might donate needed equipment to the school, or allow its employees to volunteer at the school during regular work hours. These Adopt-a-School partnerships were a strategy for building long-term relationships between businesses and schools.

Chicago's then-school superintendent, Ruth Love, led the nation with this movement to reform relationships between schools and the business community. A November 1982, article in *Time* magazine, "Education: Big Business Becomes Big Brother," reported on some of the movement's successes. The article quoted 12-year-old Anton Anderson, who was participating in Chicago's Commonwealth Edison Company Adopt-a-School program: "I know all about kilowatts and BTUs, that's British Thermal Units," Anton explained. Not only did Anton's knowledge about electricity increase, but students in his Adopt-a-School program raised their reading levels as well. Ellie McGrath and Ken Banta, authors of the *Time* article, reported that classes boosted their "reading-skill level by 14 months compared with the 8-month increase reported by other students." All told, according to McGrath and Banta, "102 companies and organizations had adopted 116 of Chicago's 604 public schools," an indication of the business community's support for the movement.

Corporate involvement with public education expanded to other school districts across the country, including the cities of Houston, Atlanta, Los Angeles, and Boston. The outcomes and benefits of involvement varied. These included field trips, as well as executives "loaned" to schools for teaching and other services. Some programs sent company employees to tutor or read to students, or to teach classes regarding the company's business or product, as with the Edison Company's teaching about BTUs. Many Adopt-A-School programs provided valuable role models and mentors for students.

Schools were indeed the primary beneficiary of Adopt-a-School programs, and yet self-interest also motivated businesses to become involved. Publicity regarding a corporation's services to schools enhanced its standing in the community and allowed it to be seen as a good corporate citizen. The services it provided to schools often changed its relationship with parents, who were also consumers of its products and services, and at the same time cultivated a relationship with future consumers.

Some CEOs also found that not only did their companies benefit from a marketing perspective, but they also gained other valuable advantages from a closer relationship with schools. Most notably, they were able to contribute to the education and development of their own future workforce. Corporate volunteers gained a first-hand understanding of their schools and customers. In speaking about the benefits of the relationship between the school and the corporate partner, Robert Manning, the division vice president for Chicago's Commonwealth Edison Company, explained, "It turned out to be a kind of Dale Carnegie course for our people."

Quoted in the *Time* magazine article, Rance Crain, editor-in-chief of *Crain's Chicago Business*, acknowledged that an element of self-interest was behind his firm's decision to teach journalism at Carl Schurz High School. But Crain defined that interest broadly: "A weak school system means weak students, and that means weak employees, weak managers—and a weak society."

Another kind of community/corporate involvement that went further than the Adopt-a-School arrangement was the Public-Private Partnership. In the 1980s, I was involved in such a program in Washington, DC (which was discussed in the previous chapter).

Also in the 1980s, still another strategy for improving what happened inside the schools grew out of the philosophy and theories of Mortimer Adler, author of *The Paideia Proposal: An Educational Manifesto*, first published on behalf of the Paideia Group by Collier Books in 1982, and in 1983 by MacMillan Publishing Company.

Mortimer Adler was a professor, philosopher, and education theorist who believed that children, being human, have a sameness. He noted that "every child has all the distinguishing properties common to all members of the species," and he believed that "children must acquire three different types of knowledge: organized knowledge, intellectual skills, and understanding of ideas and values." According to Margaret Farrand's personal biography of Mortimer Adler:

> For each of these types of knowledge, there is a different teaching style. Organized, or factual, knowledge is to be taught through lectures, intellectual skills are to be taught through coaching and supervised practice, and understanding of ideas and values are to be taught through the Socratic method of discussion and questioning. . . . For him, education should serve three purposes: to teach people how to use their leisure time well, to teach people to earn their living ethically, and to teach people to be responsible citizens in a democracy.

As a reform strategy, the Paideia model focused on a way of thinking about children's abilities and a process for teachers to deliver instruction in schools. Adler focused on a student-centered rather than teacher-centered classroom, an important element of his philosophy that led to a shift in educators' thinking. This change in thinking was the belief that all children can learn.

In 1984, in Chattanooga, Tennessee, parents and other community members, with Jack Murrah of the Lyndhurst Foundation, used the Paideia model at the Chattanooga Arts and Science School. At the height of educational reform, the Adler Paideia model fostered high expectations and a rigorous curriculum for all students. Adler believed this would mitigate against inequalities in education, a challenge that still remains, as evidenced by the re-segregation of schools and a widening achievement gap. Adler, like Dewey, recognized the relationship between democracy and education. Both believed, in Adler's words, that "vocational training, training for particular jobs, is not education of free men and women."

According to the Paideia model, schooling is only a part of education: "Education institutions, even at their best, cannot turn out fully educated men and women," wrote Adler. Yet when the Paideia model is used as the basis of *education* reform, all too often those reforms focus primarily on what happens in *schools*.

In fact, all of the reform efforts discussed above focused on what happens within schools or, in some cases, in school districts. Most of the practices tinkered with various elements of schooling rather than seeking to transform the whole system.

Professionalization, High-Stakes Tests, and Mayoral Takeovers

Over time, pushback from communities grew as people expected schools to meet more and more of their children's needs. Teachers and other school staff were overwhelmed by demands not only to meet children's academic needs, but also their psychological, disciplinary, nutritional, health, and a host of other social and economic needs.

Further complicating the problems was some districts' tendency to send mixed signals: if a child entered school unable to say the alphabet, teachers might tell parents, "You need to read to her more and teach her the alphabet"; yet later the same teacher, struggling with a large classroom of children with widely varying achievement levels, might say, "I'll teach your child to read; don't try to teach her before she comes to school." Frustration grew in both camps, as there was minimal to no significant interaction or collaboration between schools and the larger community.

Through the course of more than three decades as a teacher and administrator in public school systems, I perceived that education was becoming more and more the responsibility of professionals, with the public's role steadily decreasing. Nevertheless, in community after community, the public voiced its dissatisfaction with school performance.

Meanwhile, students were required to pass standardized tests at certain grade levels and as a high school graduation requirement. Controversy often surrounded the tests, and low scores deepened the separation and disconnect between the community and its schools. Pressure increased on teachers and school administrators, who were evaluated according to their students' and schools' performance. As a result, standardized tests frequently have become the primary focus of what was being taught.

Perhaps inevitably, allegations occasionally arose that some teachers, counselors, and principals were "cheating" by inaccurately reporting test results, in order to avoid the consequences of being identified with low scores. These negative reports further strained the relationship between the school and the community.

By the 1990s, when all efforts failed to produce acceptable test scores, some large city governments were beginning to take over entire school districts. In such mayoral takeovers, school districts were no longer independent, and superintendents were required to report to the mayor rather than the school board, which represented the community. In some instances, both superintendents and elected school boards were replaced with mayoral appointees. Such moves, clearly at odds with deeply held beliefs about local control, diminish the intended relationship of school boards to the public they represent and thus further aggravate the growing divide between schools and communities. One significant question that arises from this trend is, what are the implications for democracy when local voices are silenced in decision making for public education?

Opponents argue that whereas elected board members generally represent neighborhoods and smaller segments of the city, in school-district takeovers, a mayor is inclined to promote policies that reflect the needs of the larger city, rather than taking into consideration the needs of a local neighborhood and its schools. Furthermore, they say local board members are better able to understand resident issues and to interpret nuances that shape policies that may be missed in policies focused more broadly.

Another major issue for opponents is that policy efforts led by a big-city mayor run the risk of marginalizing neighborhood school districts with less political clout, jeopardizing, in particular, minority citizens' opportunities for self-rule.

Proponents of mayoral takeovers spotlight districtwide infrastructure, such as governance, management, and fiscal accountability. Also, frustrated with the behavior of many school board members—corruption, nepotism, conflict with superintendents and fellow board members, and a focus on personal political gain rather than the school district's progress—proponents would simply abolish school boards. Some boards, it seems, wanted to micromanage day-to-day operations and, in effect, blocked school improvement. Two superintendents I knew who actually listened and responded to parents and other segments of the community, found their boards impossible to deal with. After several years of struggling, like Sisyphus moving the boulder uphill only to watch it roll back down, they simply left their school systems. Both school districts lost real visionaries.

Opponents of mayoral takeovers generally see it as an ineffective strategy for improving schools or increasing student achievement, yet their primary focus is on the ways in which mayoral takeovers minimize political access, civic engagement, and representation of all voices. Research consistently finds little evidence that mayoral takeovers improve student achievement or fiscal efficiency. In "Looking for Leadership: Assessing the Case for Mayoral Control of Urban Schools," Frederick M. Hess reports that without a broader coalition, this governance reform strategy will not accomplish what advocates expect. Findings suggest that long-term benefits like improved student achievement are hard to pin down.

Yet Hess references Stefanie Chambers, who in her book, *Mayors and Schools: Minority Voices and Democratic Tensions in Urban Education* examines mayoral takeovers in Chicago and Cleveland. Chambers writes that student test scores did indeed improve under an appointed board, but notes also that there were fewer opportunities for grassroots participation by minority community members in the school system. Both Hess and Chambers argue that perhaps a broader coalition is necessary for school improvement, as, not surprisingly, a mayor's tendency is to look more at the bigger picture, while perhaps missing the valuable contributions made by local communities.

The Center for the Study of Social Policy surveyed what is known about various governance reforms and reported no clear evidence that mayoral takeovers improve either student achievement or school efficiency.

Education scholars Larry Cuban and Michael Usdan studied school reform in six cities and reported little evidence that mayoral control helped improve teaching, learning, or educational outcome. They did, however, find some evidence of increased city and school coordination with mayoral appointments. The point is that while city governments and school administrators communicated with each other, that communication had no measurable impact on what kids were learning.

Other researchers did, however, report successes. In their examination of the history of mayoral involvement, for example, Michael Kirst and Katrina Bulkley saw promise in what the cities of Boston and Chicago accomplished. One of their important observations was about the effect of longevity and the relationship between the mayor and superintendent. Both cities had strong mayors, and superintendents did not rotate in and out of districts as they had elsewhere— both factors that made a difference in the reforms' success. Boston's Mayor Thomas M. Menino and Superintendent Thomas Payzant were not only strong leaders, but they also served in their respective roles for a decade and had a solid working relationship.

Other evidence supports stable leadership and consistent collaboration between a mayor and superintendent as having potential to improve schools. The focus of a broad coalition among the different sectors and grassroots engagement are also important elements in the equation. Research indicates that citizens seldom elect mayors based on their role in school improvement, but education is so closely linked with a democratic society and a community's economic viability, a mayor's commitment to improving public education is clearly important.

Nashville mayor Bill Purcell, Long Beach mayor Beverly O'Neill, and San Jose mayor Ron Gonzales, for example, have all been described as using the high profile of their office to elevate the level of community concern for public education. That perhaps is the bottom line: public education must be a concern of the community-at-large. Neighborhood by neighborhood, every citizen, business, school, and community sector can contribute to education. In a democracy, the public is responsible for educating its young people.

Education Is More than Schooling

In the preceding pages I have examined many variations of "education reform." It is fair to say that the ultimate goal in nearly every case was to benefit the next generation, strengthen the community's economic viability, and ensure a decent quality of life for its citizens. The research findings, personal experiences, and other stories presented above reveal many different ways of approaching reform. They also reveal many different reasons for implementing reform in the first place: low student achievement, inadequate school financing, dysfunctional leadership and governance, a need for more or better professional-development opportunities for teachers, issues associated with desegregation plans, parent and community dissatisfaction, uneasy relationships between school districts and teachers' unions—to name a few. In nearly every instance, the approach to reforming education has specifically and singularly targeted schools, and one or a few specific aspects of schooling.

Time and again, strategies that focused on a single aspect of schools, such as governance through mayoral takeovers, for example; the organizational structure of the school, as with the "open class-room" or team-teaching; professional-development programs for teachers; or specific strategies, such as matching teaching styles with student learning styles; have failed to achieve long-term, sustainable success. What else is needed?

For some time, money has been thrown at new ideas to change schools, but the ideas have not worked to make a real difference. The achievement gap continues to grow, and student performance and scores on high-stakes tests continue to be a problem. The parental and community disconnect continues to expand. High school graduation rates have worsened in many districts. The curriculum has narrowed, primarily in response to testing requirements. I once overheard a seasoned teacher from a large Alabama school district say to a colleague, "We are told we must teach what's on the test." I was so alarmed that I turned to the two of them, apologized for overhearing, and asked her to repeat what she had said. She did, and I asked her a simple question, "Why?" She replied, "We have to get the test scores up—simple as that. Low test scores means a loss of students, and that means a loss of funds." Summing up, she added, "It is awful."

In short, reform has traveled from one element of schooling to another. As educators we have jumped on the bus for every new trend, but the ride has always been short because we keep transferring to the next bus with every new idea.

In this review and discussion of some reform efforts we can see that school reform has been narrowly focused. The underlying goal in most cases has been to transform education, yet instead it seems we tinker with changing schools and their structure, and never impact the whole of education. Schools have been bombarded with demands for change from parents, from advocates of the back-to-basics movement, from states that require every child to pass standardized exams, and the requirements of the federal government's No Child Left Behind Act.

I once heard a nationally recognized educator say that the results of high-stakes tests *need* to be accepted. She explained, in a state known for low-performing schools, "If you think young people have lost out before, you have not seen anything yet with what this will bring." She, as do I, strongly supports learning standards, high expectations for students, assessment, and accountability in teaching and learning. Yet these high-stakes tests do not seem to do what is needed. If the curriculum focus is minimized instead of broadened, with both knowledge and experiences, is that the best "education" for our young people? Overall, as a nation, we still rank lower than most industrialized countries in science, technology, engineering, and math.

Throughout this chapter I have made a distinction between "transformation" and "reform," although only a thin line may distinguish the literal meaning of the two words. In practice, a *transformation* changes all parts and relationships that are engaged in the process of educating. Transformation is integrated into the whole, reaching beyond isolated elements to create improvement in the whole. The sum of the parts of public education includes parents, teachers, principals, districtwide staff, local citizens, students, businesses, and "educating" institutions like museums and libraries. Public education, in short, is the responsibility of the public. *Reform* in practice, as described earlier, has primarily emphasized improvements in schooling. Schools are important; yet public education is more than schooling alone.

Perhaps the more narrow view of education-as-schooling results partly from a changing society, in which an increase in the mobility of families has increased the demands on schools. Schools were expected to juggle academic and skill development, while also meeting health, social service, and other changing societal needs. In effect, schools became more isolated as communities became more disconnected. At the same time, members of the community expected that schools return to the basics, rigorously discipline students, and generally meet the needs of both students and their families. The shame and blame game grew exponentially. Schools balked. Teachers asserted that they could not resolve all these issues—and teach, too. They often blamed parents for the undisciplined behavior, academic unreadiness, and poor school performance of young people. A few teachers claimed, in exasperation, that with different parents and children, they would be able to do their jobs!

Education Links Schools and Communities

The work of Lawrence Cremin, a leading 20th-century educator and historian, points out that educating takes place not only in the schools, but also beyond the schools. A former president of Teachers College of Columbia University, Cremin identified a multitude of community organizations and institutions that educate and contribute to the learning and development of youth. He also reminded us that in a democracy, public education is the responsibility of the public. If we accept this view, then we must acknowledge that reforming isolated elements is not enough to transform public education.

The John Gardner Center for Youth Development describes its work as "based on the premise that communities cannot thrive without socially engaged, successful young people," adding that "school and community go hand in hand." Yet more than at any other time in the history of public education in the United States, the term *education* has become understood as synonymous with *schooling*. This mind-set minimizes the relationship between youth, the school community, the economy, the well-being of citizens, and business. According to the website of the John Gardner Center, "When communities place youth at the center of their institutions and practices, both youth and their communities prosper."

Leading education historians and scholars, from the 19th century and into the 21st century, have addressed the relationship of public education to democracy, and the public's responsibility to education. According to scholars, such as John Dewey and Lawrence Cremin as well as professor of psychology and education Edmund Gordon and anthropologist Hervé Varenne, both of Teachers College, Columbia University, the public must be put back in public schools; we must intentionally broaden the meaning of education.

John Dewey believed there is an intimate connection between education and social action in a democracy, writing in *School and Society*, published in 1889, that "Democracy has to be born anew every generation, and education is its midwife." Dewey's theories and research pointed to schools as the "major agencies for the development of free personalities," according to David Sidorsky, also of Teachers College, in an online article, "John Dewey and Progressive Education."

In 1896, Dewey's ideas were implemented at the University of Chicago's experimental school. His ideas focused mostly on the responsibility of schools to teach students the skills necessary to live in a democracy. Among these essential skills, Dewey included problem solving, critical thinking, and active civic engagement. He believed that schools should teach students to become contributing citizens, writing, "In a complex society, ability to understand and sympathize with the operations and lot of others is a condition of common purpose which only education can procure."

Dewey felt that young people must experience compassion and an empathetic understanding for one another. These skills are central to developing what educators now call "emotional intelligence," and for living in diverse communities.

Dewey believed that students should participate in making decisions that affect their learning. He acknowledged incidental learning that occurred in daily living, yet his work was directed toward intentional learning in schools. In 1975, Lawrence Cremin published "Public Education and the Education of the Public," in the *TC Record: The Voice of Scholarship in Education*. This article, originally presented in a speech in the John Dewey Lecture Series, noted that Dewey's concept of education was rigorously comprehensive regarding what it takes for children to learn. Cremin stated that Dewey believed "the only way in which adults can constantly control the kind of education that children get is by controlling the environment in which they act, think, and feel."

John Dewey's focus was on schools' responsibility for teaching democratic practices to students. In contrast, Lawrence Cremin, who knew Dewey, emphasized the public's responsibility for education. Cremin's view of education is more comprehensive, and therefore from his perspective the role of the community is essential in the education of young people. In essence, education is both within and beyond just schooling. Given that, one might consider the question, in public education, are schools and their communities inseparable?

Lawrence Cremin was, in 1981, awarded a Pulitzer Prize in history for the second volume in his three-volume comparative history of education in the United States, entitled *American Education: The National Experience, 1783-1876*. This is perhaps the most comprehensive history of American education ever written. He also received the 1962 Bancroft Prize in American history for his book, *The Transformation of the School: Progressivism in American Education, 1876-1957.*

Cremin's philosophy of education was comprehensive and went beyond the "intentional" education provided by schools, as Dewey had described. Cremin believed agencies in the community, including museums, libraries, cultural arts centers, and countless other institutions, could play a role in educating young people. According to the *Encyclopedia of American Education*, Cremin defined education broadly, as a "deliberate, systemic and sustained effort to transmit, evoke, or acquire knowledge, values, attitudes, skills, and sensibilities, as well as any learning that results from that effort, direct or indirect, intended or unintended."

Cremin differed with Dewey in believing that incidental learning was very important, and that the family was a powerful force in the early learning of young people. He felt that education in schools allowed for more accountability, but he disagreed with Dewey that the school influence on achievement level outweighed that of the family. Of education, Cremin said, "First we must think comprehensively; second, relationally; and third, publically," meaning that "we must be aware of the public's thinking about education and public policy-making, for education goes on at a variety of levels and in a variety of places." It is clear that Lawrence Cremin, like John Dewey, saw an intricate relationship between education and democracy, but Cremin's more comprehensive view was highly inclusive, extending the reach of education far beyond the boundaries of the school, locally, statewide, regionally, federally, and internationally. In Cremin's view, citizens have an important role in educating and developing young people.

David Brown, a Kettering Foundation associate, wrote in an unpublished article that the theories of Cremin broadened the definition of education and reflected the essence of Kettering Foundation's ongoing research. This connection with the foundation's research, Brown continues, is particularly found when Cremin asked the questions, "What knowledge should 'we the people' hold in common? What values? What skills? What sensibilities?"

In fact the foundation's community educators research was influenced considerably by Lawrence Cremin's assertions about education. Although Cremin passed away in 1990, others have continued with this thinking about education into the 21st century. Hervé Varenne and Edmund Gordon continue to identify Cremin's definition of education as one that clarifies the comprehensive meaning of education.

Given the focus of Kettering Foundation's research—What does it take to make democracy work as it should?—I find that Cremin and Dewey provide a foundation for the findings associated with the community educators study. Although Cremin expanded Dewey's definition of education, both of them understood the intricate connection between education and democracy, a connection that demands a definition of education that goes beyond schooling.

Such a definition of education opens the door to the kind of citizen involvement that both relies on and strengthens relationships within the community. Building such networks and relationships is at the heart of many of the programs represented in the community educators research. In a survey conducted for that project, adult-youth relationships and social development were identified most frequently as important features in the community educators programs. Among the features that respondents mentioned are mentoring, character development, improved relationships and understanding between adults and youth, social-skill development, tutoring, and teaching cultural identity and community values. In an after-school program in Silver Spring, Maryland, college students and other adults serve as volunteer mentors who meet with young people once or twice a week. These citizens work in collaboration with teachers who provide tutoring for the students. Frank Chisley, director of the Ambassadors Investing in Mentoring (AIM) program in Silver Spring, says that students' relationships with adults made a difference in young people's lives, and that reports from the school indicate that the behavior of participants improved. Finally, although mentoring was the primary focus of this program, improved academic performance was also reported.

Kettering Foundation research on the achievement gap, from 2007-2009, focused on the wide disparities in young people's academic performance. A key finding was that the term *achievement gap* may be primarily the language of professional educators describing poor test scores or school performance. However, citizen participants were more concerned about closing "other gaps" that make a difference in what young people bring to school, even before any measurement of achievement has been determined. Gaps in socioeconomic conditions, health, "lap reading" time, language development, self-esteem, social skills, sense of belonging, self-confidence, and other factors must also be closed. In fact, many education researchers say that until these gaps are closed, there is little sense in trying to address the achievement gap. I say, both must be addressed simultaneously and continuously. The social and economic gaps are embedded in the cultural patterns and the quality of home and community life. A start-and-stop process is not the solution.

In the community educators research, we found committed individual citizens, organizations, and associations engaged in after-school programs that focused on closing such gaps. They are making a long-term investment in the lives of youth. Through experiences in settings as diverse as horse farms, firehouses, community centers, museums, cultural art centers, churches, and numerous other public spaces, citizens volunteer their time, energy, and talents to closing the gaps. As Edmund Gordon has noted in his work at Columbia, these community educators believe that the focus of education should be on the development of the whole child. Community educators further report that a community focus on youth development has been a source for building positive community development.

John McKnight is cofounder of the Asset-Based Community Development Institute, an organization that describes itself as being "at the center of a large and growing movement that considers local assets as the primary building blocks of sustainable community development." McKnight has authored several influential books on community building, including *Building the Community from the Inside Out*, coauthored with John Kretzmann and published in 1993.

Much of McKnight's research describes the mind-set of the 1960s, when community reform was heightened as a result of the societal changes that followed the Civil Rights Movement and other social changes of that time. The accepted view of citizens was as consumers of services, and the emphasis of community building was on responding to the needs and deficits of individuals and groups in the community. McKnight wrote that during this period, there was a spirit of reform that would change American cities and create better schools, medical systems, social-service systems, governments, and criminal justice systems. In this client-centered thinking, according to McKnight, it was assumed that "the key to reforming these systems was adequate funding . . . modern technology, personnel training, and management methods."

McKnight pointed out, "Our unrecognized premise was that well-being was determined by the sum of a resident's consumption of services. But could service consumption by clients really change individual behavior, social relationships, the physical and economic environment? Was there any place on the map for the residents and their own actions?"

Not unlike the discussion of education reform earlier in this chapter, community reform was expected to change the whole, while actually addressing only a few aspects of the community. McKnight recognized that achieving change in a community required more than reform. It is my understanding of McKnight's work, then, that true community change requires a transformation of the entire system's attitudes, relationships, and mind-sets—it requires more than moving the furniture around the room. And community, of course, includes schools—which leads me to the question, is this what Bob Cornett meant, when he said we cannot "fix" schools unless we "fix" the community?

I'm reminded of Fats Waller singing the old folk song "Dem Bones": "The foot bone's connected to the leg bone, the leg bone's connected to the knee bone, the knee bone's connected to the thigh bone. . . . It's easy to connect those dry bones." (He always ended the song with a laugh.) It certainly wasn't Waller's intention, but the song is a perfect analogy for the connectedness and interdependence of schools to the community, the community to schools—and both to the broader meaning of education. The connectedness involves individual and collective citizens; both those in the mainstream and those who are frequently marginalized. It involves for-profit and not-for-profit institutions, both public and private, large and small. It involves civic and social organizations, government agencies, and all manner of associations. All of these are necessary participants in discussions to bring about the kind of paradigm shift necessary for transformation.

For example, one community educator told about a 2007 series of communitywide dialogues about youth violence in Suffolk, Virginia. Afterward, members of the police and fire departments contributed to a solution by responding collectively, both in their institutional roles and as citizens of the community. They collaborated with local schools, and jointly implemented an after-school youth-development program, the Youth Public Safety Academy, through which young people met regularly with both firefighters and police officers at the firehouse.

Their program built relationships between youth and caring adults, often over spaghetti dinners. These informal gatherings helped young people begin to develop an awareness of career opportunities, as they garnered a better understanding of the work of firefighters and police officers. In turn, the fire- and crime-fighters gained a better understanding of the youth and what life was like for them.

On one site visit to this firehouse in Suffolk, I asked a police officer why he had chosen to participate in the program. In a voice that expressed deep concern and compassion, he told me, "I often encounter some of these youth in the community when they get into difficulty. I want them to get to know me as a person and to see that I'm no different from them, that I am there to help and support them. I also want to know who they are. I want to get to know them before there is a problem. Maybe that way the problem could be prevented." As these new relationships form and have positive results, they benefit youth and adult participants and the community. In Suffolk, these civil servants are an asset in the community not only for the service they provide through their jobs, but they are also using their talents and skills in a youth-development program.

The community as an asset for resolving its own problems, as John McKnight describes it, is most effective when the individual and collective mind-set of the community moves from seeing citizens as clients, consumers, and recipients of services, to citizens who take ownership and responsibility for the issues and challenges in their community. Among the most important of the issues and challenges is education. The key, according to McKnight, is to focus on assets rather than deficiencies.

In *Building Communities from the Inside Out*, McKnight and his colleague John Kretzmann describe the limitations of institutional reform:

> Unfortunately, we spend so much of our effort, attention, and resources on institutional reform that we usually ignore the inventive—and often more effective—efforts of citizens in associations as they grapple with the questions of neighborhood change. . . . Citizens are inventing, creating, and discovering new paths for raising young people, revitalizing their economy, overcoming discrimination, promoting health, and ensuring security. These efforts, however, fall largely under the radar of most researchers, marketers, governments, funders, and the media. Nonetheless, citizens are persistently at work creating new ways to meet those human needs resulting from the inherent limits of large institutions and systems.

In the community educators research, we learned that individuals, associations, organizations, and government agencies were applying their strengths, skills, experiences, and talents to youth development. Their individual and collective resources are human capital and local assets that strengthen youth and build community. Community educators from different communities gathered to tell stories of the benefit and value of human capital for educating and developing youth, and they reported that their programs had made a positive difference in the lives of both youth and adult participants.

Defining *Community*
During the course of this work it became apparent that the word

community was unclear and took on many different connotations. In an attempt to clarify the term, in the Kettering Foundation's Public-Public Education Workgroup we have explored a number of definitions. Two definitions discussed among Kettering colleagues may offer some insight into how we use the term in the community educators study. According to one definition, "a community is a continuous multilevel source for collective action." A second, offered by David Mathews, president of the Kettering Foundation, says that "community is a group that comes together and acts effectively on their collective well-being." Both definitions are useful for describing the endeavors we called "community" in the community educators study. Clearly in many instances the work of citizens was a multilevel resource acting on behalf of youth. At the same time, programs collaborated with others and created partnerships to take action that benefited their collective well-being.

In the community educators research we noticed we were using the word *community* to discuss the different types of programs participating. Although the youth population was diverse economically, ethnically, and so on, nearly all the programs operated in a defined geographic area. Most of them were inspired and initiated by civic, social, or nonprofit organizations, and organized by mayors, government agencies, private independent efforts, museums, cultural art centers, and others. Although the size and "flavor" of community varies, all of these citizens are committed to action that achieves positive growth and development of youth in a particular locality.

There are many ways to look at "community," so it is important for readers of this book to understand that in the community educators study, we have used and understood community in more than one way. A community effort may be described as individuals working with a select youth population, such as one identified with a single church community, a neighborhood, a specific school community, or other such entity. Two cities represented in the community educators study—Albion, Michigan, and St. Louis Park, Minnesota—engaged citizens communitywide, including schools and all sectors to focus on educating and developing youth.

In the following chapters you will find more information about the community educators research, including program descriptions, as well as obstacles and challenges the programs face in their work. You will also find information about findings, lessons learned, and implications for further research.

After reading this book, perhaps you and others may choose to explore the possibilities for youth in your community. You may want to invite your neighbors, your work colleagues, your book club, or other citizens in your community, individually and collectively, to read the study and consider how best to discuss and deliberate about youth concerns in your community. As you weigh alternative solutions that seem best suited for your area or neighborhood, you may find it helpful to keep in mind the four underlying questions behind this study:

- How is my community a resource for the growth, development, and education of the next generation?
- What makes democracy work in our community?
- What is the relationship between democracy, education, and the public in our community?
- What is the relationship between school and community; and what examples or stories, in our community, reflect how that relationship impacts youth education and development and community development?

Guided in part by these questions, you may want to identify the talents, human resources, and additional assets available in your community. You may rediscover the value and benefits that citizen engagement and community ownership of education bring to youth and community development.

===========A STORY FROM THE FIELD===========

Fostering a Culture of Youth Leadership

Patrick Johnson

"There's nowhere to go and nothing to do." That's what my peers told me when I interviewed them as a youth planner for the City of Hampton, Virginia, in 1995. I was one of two high school seniors hired by the city to develop the youth component of the 2010 Comprehensive Plan, and the interviews were part of our research. Over and over, teenagers said, "We need a safe place to hang out and have fun. Not a typical recreation center, but a teen center with a full set of services and activities designed for youth."

My colleague and I dutifully recorded the dream on our flip charts, wondering if it wasn't mostly a pipe dream. Still, we worked to convince civic leaders that teenagers really wanted such a place and would use such a place, and that the city should invest in the vision even though teenagers can't vote and pay little in taxes. After many conversations and plenty of tough questions, we were surprised and thrilled when the City Council agreed to include a teen center in the city's master plan for 2010. As a high school senior in 1997, the year 2010 seemed like a lifetime away.

When we graduated, my colleague and I turned over our work to other students, and we wished them well. Indeed, over the next 15 years many teams of young people worked to implement the youth component of the Comprehensive Plan, eventually forming the Hampton Youth Commission as a way to provide institutional continuity for youth leadership. After getting the City Council to agree to the vision, the group's next step was to address concerns about safety and transportation, which included reviewing bus routes, interviewing school division leaders and staff from the Parks and Recreation Department, and talking with school resource officers and police officers about security plans. Once these plans were presented to the City Council, the final step was to convince taxpayers that a teen center was a good investment, especially for a city with increasing numbers of senior citizens. To do this, youth leaders developed an interactive website that included a virtual tour of the proposed teen center, and made presentations to civic associations and other community groups.

Finally, the City of Hampton invested $2.8 million to purchase a former health and fitness center that would be converted into the Hampton Teen Center. After 15 years, the teen center dream became reality on opening day in August 2009. The facility includes meeting rooms, a lounge, cyber café, creativity center, dance studio, recording studio, and half-court basketball and recreation space. In order to maximize use, Hampton City Schools, in partnership with Communities in Schools (an Arlington-based dropout prevention organization), provides an alternative education program for teens at the center during the day—operating both an early day and twilight program. In addition, teens utilize the space as an after-school site. Through the support of the federal AmeriCorps program, students from Christopher Newport University provide staff support and organize community-service projects, special events, and social gatherings for teens.

Looking back, I am amazed by the community leaders who were willing to listen to our concerns, give us a seat at the table, and support us in achieving our dreams. Alternatives, Inc., a community-based youth-development nonprofit, provided training and organizational support to each new generation of youth leaders. Each year, teens would receive civic leadership training that included concepts used in the corporate world, such as Seven Habits and Creative Competencies of Leadership.

Recognizing the value of such training, Hampton City Schools provided elective credits for students who participated in the training, thereby adding academic status to community-based training. Alternatives, Inc., in partnership with the City of Hampton, also facilitated workshops for adults throughout the community, some of which were cofacilitated by teens. Through these efforts the community began to see youth as leaders who could address community issues with creativity and vitality.

As one of the youth who first heard this dream and scribbled it on a flip chart in a high school library, I see the teen center as both an impressive and surprising achievement. Today, young people on the Teen Center Advisory Board and the Hampton Youth Commission continue to advocate for their concerns and for the continued support of the teen center, even in a poor economy. Moreover, Hampton continues to foster a culture of youth leadership through ongoing youth-adult partnerships and opportunities for youth civic engagement. After 15 years, young people in Hampton now have somewhere to go and something to do. In a greater sense, the young people who are influenced by the youth leadership culture in Hampton have the skills and confidence to go anywhere and do anything.

Patrick Johnson—is a husband and father who currently lives in Frenchtown, New Jersey. He is the pastor of the Frenchtown Presbyterian Church and is active in the local community. He also teaches courses in practical theology at Princeton Theological Seminary, in Princeton, New Jersey, where he is completing his doctorate in practical theology. Patrick is a member of the Lions Club International, the National Communication Association, and the Academy of Homiletics. While growing up in Hampton, Virginia, he was active in the City's Youth Civic Engagement Initiative.

CHAPTER THREE

COMMUNITY EDUCATORS FOCUS ON YOUTH DEVELOPMENT

Above all, people educate themselves with people who have little if any direct authority over them, and who have no specialized expertise either on curriculum or pedagogy.

Hervé Varenne

This chapter describes in some detail the emergence and evolution of the community educators research. Working with a group of Kettering Foundation researchers and associates, it includes a description of our methodology and research process, as well as reporting from the research conversation participants' own words. It also includes some of what we have learned through other data collection methods, specifically, site visits and a community educators survey.

KF research into community educators programs has been interactive and reflective, and as the three-year project has come to a close, we hope to continue that interaction and reflection. With this publication we offer information about the programs we've studied. We hope to inspire local conversations among other individuals, institutions, organizations, and communities about the role of the public in developing and educating youth.

As you read, reflect on opportunities for youth development in your own community, as well as on what role and talents you bring—or might bring—to efforts at providing such opportunities. You might also go a little further and ask yourself, *How do youth development and education help strengthen, more broadly, community development and democracy? Or do they? How does "the public" in your community take ownership and, ultimately, responsibility for the long-term development of your youth?*

Methodology for Community Educators Study
Literature Search

To identify programs for possible inclusion in community educators research conversations, we began with a limited and selected literature search on the role of the community in education. We read publications of associations and organizations affiliated with youth development, such as The Links, Incorporated and the National League of Cities; articles by academics and researchers, including John Dewey, Lawrence Cremin, Hervé Varenne, Edmund Gordon, and others; and we reviewed earlier research from the Kettering Foundation and talked with a number of foundation staff and associates, including the foundation's president, David Mathews. Ultimately we compiled a list of community educators programs, some operated through private or public organizations or associations, as well as those initiated and run by community leaders and other individuals.

Interviews

By telephone and through site visits, I talked with individuals involved with some of the programs we identified. These interviews provided some insight regarding the kinds of problems these programs were trying to solve, as well as a means by which to narrow the search for research conversation participants.

Criteria for Participation in the Community Educators Research

The next step was to establish a list of basic criteria in order to select programs for the study. Primarily, we were interested in programs that operated outside of regular school hours and that were focused on "educating" young people. We looked for after-school programs that supported youth from kindergarten through 12th grade, or some subset of that range, including programs that had emerged organically out of some informal relationship, as well as those created and structured intentionally in response to a particular need. We looked for programs that had been initiated by individuals or groups of individuals, and for those that were part of local civic organizations or local chapters of national organizations like Girls Inc., 100 Black Men, 4-H Clubs, and member cities of the National League of Cities. Based on these criteria, we identified a number of programs for inclusion in the research, and once we had invited individuals from several of these programs, we asked them to recommend others for us to invite.

Research Conversations

Altogether we convened six research conversations at the Kettering Foundation in Dayton, Ohio, all of which followed an inquiry-and-discussion model through which participants reflected on questions pertinent to the study. The conversations took place during one-day workshops over the course of three years, with a different set

of participants for each. At our invitation, several research participants provided written reflections on their research conversations,
including any lessons they may have learned from the experience.

The programs represented in our research conversations were
founded and implemented by individuals, organizations, and, in
some cases, municipalities led by local mayors or city managers, all
of whom were dedicated to a positive future for young people. They
saw a need, and they responded. In nearly every case these individuals reached out to create partnerships and collaborate with other
citizens, sectors, or institutions, including schools, local chapters
of national organizations, 501(c)(3) nonprofit institutions, civic and
social organizations, and municipal governments. Only one of the
programs was actually housed in a school building and operated during school hours; although the rest were after-school programs, some
of them collaborated in one way or another with local schools.

Participants in the community educators workshops played
a number of different roles in their organizations, including both
leadership and staff positions. They were founders, volunteers, board
members, CEOs, directors, and program coordinators; together, they
brought a considerable diversity of perspectives to our research.

A few participants led or coordinated communitywide programs
that convened stakeholders to address strategies for youth development in their community. Nevertheless, we noticed that for the most
part, program leaders did not know each other even when they came
from the same local area. A few participants knew each other from
previous grant involvement and recognition award programs, but
they had not necessarily worked together.

Online Survey

In addition to the qualitative data we gathered through the community educators research conversations, we also gathered data
through an online community educators survey. A number of survey
respondents were also participants in the research conversations,
while some were community educators who otherwise had not been
a part of Kettering Foundation's community educators research.
Altogether we invited 46 individuals to respond, and of those, 34 (74

percent) did so. Our intention through the online survey was to learn about the community's capacity to educate, to find out where such education is occurring and by whose efforts, and to further document the impact of citizens engaged in youth-development efforts.

The questionnaire utilized closed-ended questions, including "select all that apply" checklists, True/False questions, and "select only one" response options, as well as open-ended questions that allowed respondents to elaborate on their answers. An independent researcher, Sharon Newbill, of Folkstone: Evaluation Anthropology, applied both quantitative and qualitative analysis for a comprehensive and meaningful interpretation of the data. (For a complete description of the data analysis and interpretation, see the Appendix.)

Research Questions

Most Americans recognize that self-rule—government of the people, by the people, for the people—is the most important pillar of democracy. Less obvious, perhaps, is the key role that education plays in that democracy: as John Dewey noted more than 100 years ago—and as we have already mentioned— "Democracy has to be born anew every generation, and education is its midwife." The community educators research suggests an examination of the connections between education, democracy, and the role of the community, a connection that has long been an important focus of the Kettering Foundation's research. Yet for several decades now, reports have indicated that the public feels it has little or no role in, or responsibility for, educating our country's young people.

In short, the relationship between the public and public schools is estranged, with the two separated by conflicting perceptions of who "owns" education, of who is responsible for educating. As David Mathews writes in *Reclaiming Public Education by Reclaiming Our Democracy*:

> This is not an issue of whether people are confident that these institutions are doing a good job, feel close to them, and would pay taxes for their support. Ownership is a more fundamental issue: When people drive by a schoolhouse, will they say "this is

our school" or only "that's *the* school"? What they say will influence the future of public education in America.

With this relationship between democracy and education in mind, we formulated several research questions as the cornerstone of the community educators investigation:

- How are community educators programs changing the perception that only schools educate—to an understanding that education can occur and *does* occur beyond schools?
- *Who* educates, what do they do, and why? What challenges and obstacles do they encounter?
- To what extent does youth development contribute to community development? To what extent do after-school community educators programs restore public ownership and give citizens a renewed sense of their role in public education?
- Are communities a resource for educating youth? Do members of the community see themselves as such? What specific resources—such as public spaces, health facilities, arts organizations, and the skills of individual citizens— can be tapped?

Ordinary People, Extraordinary Results

In the community educators research, we encountered a number of innovative after-school efforts intended to make a difference for youth. The programs had many commonalities, although they ranged from communitywide undertakings to formal and informal programs provided by individuals or a variety of organizations and institutions. Nearly all the youth-development programs operated after school and were led and directed by men and women dedicated to developing the next generation of contributing citizen leaders. Staff and volunteers in community educators programs are not necessarily professional educators; they are ordinary human beings creating extraordinary results. Programs involved in the community educators research are creating positive youth development that engenders positive community development.

Youth get to know adults as mentors, supporters, and role models, and they expect to develop social and life skills, self-management, and emotional intelligence. They also participate in experiences that teach them to make wise choices and decisions. These youth-development programs provide learning experiences that help them develop and increase their self-esteem. They learn about new possibilities from adult role models and from each other. Many program directors and survey respondents told stories of young people gaining confidence, trying new things, and developing public speaking and communication skills.

One respondent to the community educators survey shared the story of a young person who had made a positive life change:

> One of our mentees brought a friend of his to our program, and his friend lived in a situation whereby his mother, who was a drug user, would be gone for days and he was left with no food or utilities. We provided the new student with groceries and some new clothing. He continued to attend our mentoring classes and his grades made a sharp improvement. We asked the student what had made him turn his grades around and he replied, "No one ever cared before."

Some may think this was a "small thing," but to this young man it was huge to have someone demonstrate they cared about him. Keeping promises, being there, made a difference. In the community educators programs, we noticed that just wanting youngsters to accomplish and succeed was not enough. It seems that when care was demonstrated repeatedly and consistently, it made a difference. In the case of this young man, that demonstration inspired a change in student performance, and probably much more.

Program after program reported experiences and outcomes for young people who benefitted from caring and supportive relationships. A middle school student in a Maryland community educators program participated twice a week, working one day with the teacher-tutors employed by the program and the second day with a mentor who is a volunteer from the business sector. The youth enjoyed the program, particularly spending time with his mentor, who provided the young man with an important male role model. The young man said he liked having a mentor, and that he could talk with his mentor about his feelings and what concerned him. This youngster had a history of being to himself and quiet, yet he began to open up to an individual he respected and with whom he met only once a week.

Relationships and Resources

Human resources and collaborative relationships seemed to be the dominant attribute among the community educators programs. These program features had a positive impact on youth accomplishments. Although citizens often disagreed and were emotional about what should be done about schools, teachers, and the school system, they seemed to rally behind the idea of out-of-school youth-development and education programs. It appears that the polarization about problems with schooling was diminished. Citizens seemed to move beyond traditional ethnic, racial, religious, and economic barriers, with the focus on youth development and education rather than on schooling. When youth development and education are the focus, it seems that these barriers collapse. Citizens appear to rally and come together to contribute.

Citizen educators are building relationships across many traditional boundaries that separate different groups. As youth become civic learners, leaders, and political activists, and as they expand their understanding of others, they become more confident in settings other than those with which they are familiar. Young people also explore different career possibilities that may be new to them and raise their level of aspiration for their future.

Shared Responsibility for Educating Youth

Who is responsible for educating the next generation of Americans? Many of us would say schools are the dominant source of education. As previously stated, education and schools are often treated as the same, as if they were synonymous. Nearly every conversation that begins discussing education dramatically limits the discussion to a single component, schools, as if that is the only place for learning. Rarely does the discussion expand education to broader perimeters, nor does it validate that learning takes place in many dimensions of a community, including the home. This general way of thinking about education limits the meaning of education. Parents are the first teachers, along with neighbors, peers, church, and a plethora of experiences and other institutions that contribute to what a child knows before the professional educator has contact with him or her.

I can remember teachers over the last several decades who have been frustrated with what they felt were unreasonable requirements and demands for schools to provide additional services and programs for youth. Many expressed concern that these expectations prevented them from doing their job, teaching. As the demands on teachers and schools increased, many felt unable to teach students the academics *and* meet all of society's needs, including babysitting, providing social services, and meeting health needs.

Schools and teachers are responsible for the knowledge and academic skills required to develop competence in young people, and they can engender a love for learning. Schools are not exempt from developing social skills and emotional intelligence or from matching learning and teaching styles, developing curriculum, and providing individualized instruction. These elements of schooling are incorporated in planning for instruction and teaching students.

Yet teachers, like the community educators, say they are committed to meeting the needs of the whole child. *Is the education of the whole child the purview of a single institution or entity—or is this a principle that can be embraced by all and implemented through collaboration and partnerships?* Teachers are not the only ones stating they cannot meet all of the current needs of their students as well as the demands of the community, state departments of education, and federal policies. Rather, parents and others in the community, including the business sector, have lamented this same concern—even when pushing for the schools to do more. We noticed that research in education is also addressing this issue.

A recent PBS program, *NewsHour*, anchored by Gwen Ifill, discussed current research, referred to as the American Graduate Project, which was conducted by Civic Enterprises. Ifill interviewed John Bridgeland, president and CEO of Civic Enterprises, who told her that the Civic Enterprises research affirms that teachers cannot be social workers, counselors, social-service coordinators, and so on and still fulfill their teaching responsibilities for academic knowledge and skills development. Bridgeland's comments indicate that it will take citizens, business leaders, students, educators, nonprofit organizations, and others to rebuild a broken system of education.

Community educators programs, like those in this study, are already engaged, after school, in the kind of endeavors reported in the Civic Enterprises research. This finding substantiates that to educate and develop young people requires more than schooling alone. Perhaps the Civic Enterprises research, along with the existing community educators efforts, will raise an even greater recognition that the community is a resource and the public has a responsibility to engage in the development and education of youth.

Education and learning include schools, families, and the many different dimensions and sectors of the community. To think of education as schooling alone limits the possibilities for what roles community resources may play in the learning and development of young people.

In some communities, such as those represented in the community educators study, it is clear that citizens and youth-development programs are educating young people. They are mentoring, tutoring, and helping youth to build character, develop self-esteem, and learn valuable social and leadership skills. *How* are they doing it? They are educating by using a wide variety of community resources and facilities. They are collaborating and building relationships and partnerships among the different sectors of the community, including schools. Community educators reported their predominant resource is human capital.

There is no single model for such programs, but virtually all of them could be described as facilitating the development of the whole child. Community educators noted that their whole-child approach is valuable for providing learning experiences and social-skills development. These are considered to be necessary prerequisites for successful academic performance.

In the community educators research conversations, participants repeatedly conveyed that among the keys to success are opportunities for young people to recognize and embrace their individual and cultural identity. Mary K. Boyd, a former public school administrator and community leader, noted that "cultural knowledge and identity raise the level of self-esteem, critical thinking, participating in community, valuing and taking responsibility for one's own education, and making good choices." Others also reported that it is important for youth to see themselves as a resource and an asset, to themselves, to other youth, and to their communities.

In our research conversations and in the survey, community educators shared the "problems" that their programs are attempting to solve. These issues primarily focus on youth, their communities, and the relationship between the youth and their communities. Some programs offer an alternative for young people who do not conform to school norms or may have been expelled from school.

In addition, programs often work in collaboration with youth to resolve a community and youth-related issue, such as youth violence, or to encourage political activism among young people. In other instances the programs address character, career alternatives, and leadership development. Some programs aim to increase high school graduation rates, improve readiness for and access to college, and expose youth to positive safety role models (e.g. police and firefighters). In some instances programs are encouraging youth to make positive choices rather than choosing to be in gangs.

Some youth may have a need to express themselves, be appreciated, and be validated. Some need to interact with a positive role model, have someone to talk with and listen to them. For others, it may be the assurance of a meal. Others may have been involved in some type of anti-social behavior and need assistance to get back on track.

Generally, activities that community educators use to promote youth learning are experiential; that is, they provide youth with opportunities for learning by doing. Citizen-led programs for youth development are not intended to criticize or compete with schools, but rather to provide learning that supports the development and interests of the whole child. Given that both school and community are concerned with the whole child, is it possible that the community's learning experiences might be complementary to those of the schools? If the importance of educating and developing the whole child is an authentic mutual concern shared by members of the community and professional educators, then this idea may be a powerful vehicle for joint consideration and collaboration. Both the school and the community envision this generation and those to follow becoming competent, confident, adult citizens. Youth in community educators programs have an opportunity to engage in community activities, to bring their voices forward and to be heard. They provide solutions for youth issues and participate in ways that support community development.

Citizen educators are dedicated to the future of young people as well as community viability. These citizens say they want to make a difference in the lives of youth. They are passionate, and many have also struggled with the same issues faced by the young people their programs serve. Local citizens are volunteers in each of these programs. In the community educators study, there was only one program that operated in classrooms at a school. Sharon Richardson, president of the Newport News chapter of The Links, Incorporated, shared that in an ongoing project that has existed for several years, a collaborative relationship with the teachers and the school has been highly successful. In this example, citizen educators worked directly with students in the classroom. The remaining programs in the community educators study operated after school.

Kathy Johnson, executive director of Alternatives, Inc., a Hampton, Virginia, program, noted that it is passion that inspires citizens to this work: "Informal educators and supportive adults who serve in an educational role with young people share a deep sense of 'call.'" Kathy continued, "Imparting their knowledge, wisdom, and expertise to the next generation is part of their molecular make-up and identity. While it may not be their job or profession, it is clearly their avocation." In my conversations with other community educators,

I have found that a passion to change the status quo seems to be a driving force.

When asked about this passion in one research conversation, citizen educators participating in the community educators study thought about the meaning of education, and its roots in the Latin word *educare*, meaning "to bring out from within." Many of these participants were founders and directors of their programs, and in their passion for the young people and the work they do, it was evident that the intention was to draw out the personal best and to empower and inspire young people to succeed.

This emphasis on educating is comprehensive and not limited to the pursuit of academic knowledge and skills. This is not to diminish the importance and value of academic achievement and skills development. Rather, these programs raise our level of awareness of how important the development of personal assets, social skills, and other attributes are for youth. This closes a gap between their readiness to learn and their academic success.

None of the community educators who participated in this study pointed to academics as the focus of their mission. It was a by-product of the entire experience and therefore an unintended benefit. Although tutoring was a feature in a number of programs, the primary focus was on social, cultural, civic, character, and relational development. These programs address the many different dimensions of youth, in order to help them become successful and contributing citizens. However, participants noted that academic and school performance often improved among youth in their programs.

Later in this chapter, community educators describe, in their own voices, the youth-development and education programs involved in the community educators study. Notice the ways in which they target needs applicable to the development of the whole child. Through the voices of participants, you will witness what these programs are about, what they do, the impact they have, and common themes among them. Notice the significance attributed to relationships, as they are creating social change. As you read, consider the role of the public.

The impact of these programs points to social change in the community. The 1995–2005 Healing the Heart of Diversity (HHD)

Retreat Seminars reported that sustainable social change includes transforming policies, practices, and patterns, as well as attitudes, ways of thinking, speaking, and how we relate to others. Healing the Heart of Diversity, a social-change process that I founded and directed, was implemented nationally with the support of the Fetzer Institute, the Ford Foundation, the Hewlett Packard Corporate Foundation, and the David and Lucile Packard Foundation. In this case, transformation refers to a shift in our mind-set about education and how we relate to those who educate. Further, the HHD study reported that choice is the key to change, and therefore transformation will not occur unless the citizens and educators choose to change.

> **I**s a shift in thinking about educating youth, or a new paradigm for education underway? What is missing? What is changing in the way we define and understand education? What about a shift to thinking more comprehensively, relationally, and publicly?

The director of one program in southeast Virginia submitted this reflection as a follow-up to her participation in a research conversation:

> When communities invest institutions of public education with the sole responsibility for academic outcomes, opportunities for informal education that organically occur within neighborhoods, churches, and community-based organizations lose "visibility." Loss of visibility and perceived value weakens the overall social sector, leaves formal academic institutions with unrealistic community expectations and leaves communities frustrated with outcomes indicative of troubled youth.

Community Educators: In Their Own Words

Participants in the research conversations offer the best descriptions of their programs, what they do, who they serve, and the impact they have had in the community. In the following statements, participants describe the quality, vision, and outcomes of their programs. Their statements also reveal the dedication and commitment they have to young people and the passion they have for their work.

As you read, consider the stories, descriptions, and comments participants share. Notice what, if any, may have relevance for you and your community. Consider individuals or organizations you know with whom you may choose to share this work and discuss how, or whether, it may be relevant for your community. *To what extent are there insights for your consideration to broaden the scope of who educates in your community?* Following their community educators research conversations, a number of participants contributed written reflections on their own programs. Some of them provided a broad explanation of the work they do, while others described a notable experience or a particular child whom they had encountered through their work. A few of their comments are selected and presented here. Research conversation participants were informed that their comments would be shared and are therefore identified. The survey respondents, however, are not identified, in order to maintain ano-nymity as promised.

Who Are the Community Educators?

Most of the participants in the community educators research did not initially think of themselves as "educators." In those cases when they did see themselves as such, educating was just one of many roles they played. Taken as a whole, community educators are people who do ordinary things, with extraordinary results for the youths in their programs. The official titles of participants in the community educators research included government employee, firefighter, police officer, mayor, teacher, and business owner—among others—but when asked in the survey, they described themselves, for example, as "youth-development professional," "counselor," " a church leader catching those that fall through the gaps," "adult ally; collaborator," "mentoring expert/educator/leader," "a caring adult," "champion and challenger," " youth worker," and "community servant and com-munity learner (my job is to learn from the community)."

Once the idea of "community educators" was introduced, partici-pants in this research came to see themselves that way. They did not, however, see themselves as a substitute for professional educators.

As participant Stephanie Burch, a police officer in Virginia, describes their role, "We are community educators, designed to supplement, and not supplant the school system."

What Do They Do?

Participants in the community educators study began to discuss what they actually do in their programs, they named a number of activities that could be considered as educating. Survey respondents, for example, noted the following as features of their programs: "college preparatory learning," "leadership development," "research, arts, and community engagement," "educational support," "social justice education," "collective leadership development," "asset building," and "social learning."

When asked to describe the focus of their programs, respondents mentioned "prevention, intervention, and suppression," "using historical cultural positives to create concept of 'global' citizen," "building the capacity of youth as leaders in their community to make change," "outreach for underserved population," "to develop life skills as well as environmental stewardship," "youth participatory action research," "food program for youth," "youth development," "college prep," "improving the community," "building a sense of community and offering learning opportunities," "college access," "both mentoring and academic support of the mentee," and "community youth asset-building initiative."

It is notable that even when they used the word *education*, these community educators tended to use it outside of the context of schooling. They focused repeatedly on education as it relates to developing the whole child, rather than as a means to specific academic achievement. "Learning," as one survey respondent wrote, "is about developing the whole child, not just a classroom curriculum on specific subjects." Community educators, as Becky Cooper noted, are "transforming lives through the power of human relationships."

Of course, even if academic achievement is not the sole focus of community educators work, it is certainly an important part of it. In our research, in fact, we found repeatedly that the programs' whole-child approach is quite effective at impacting young people's academic achievement. As Judy Heyboer explains, "Addressing the whole child—from providing a sense of history, to providing a full belly, to providing opportunities to progress beyond required schooling to higher level education—is a role that only the community can play."

Several survey respondents pointed to their programs' role in making education relevant to young people. One mentioned "the need for all children to be educated to a level that opens doors for employment and civic engagement," while another pointed to "the reality that education systems have historically benefited only a portion of our society." Community educators reported tangible academic results for youth who might otherwise have fallen through the cracks of the traditional school system.

Through one program, "students expelled from the regular school system continued learning and completed a G.E.D., high school diploma. . . . Mentoring and time spent outside of school had an impact on academic achievement." Another survey respondent points to the results of one-on-one tutoring:

> We have demonstrated youth ability to achieve academically. For example, children in our eight-week reading instruction/ tutorial program demonstrate an average of a 2 to 5 level increase in reading levels and reading skill sets. A majority of the children enter our reading program reading below grade level.

Sometimes the connection between community educators and schools is simple and direct: "We have been able to help youth get back into school and stay in school." In several cases, the focus on education does not end with high school. One survey respondent described a program that involves college students as mentors and role models. The program's goal is to keep young people "doing what is expected of them by going to school and being respectful towards family, friends, and their community. The college mentors are a great help in making sure the youth get a small taste of college life, have field trips to local universities, and attend educational workshops."

Yet another survey respondent underscored the vital connection between their program and education, by noting how they measure success. "We measure our impact in four ways," this respondent wrote: "Dropout reduction, high school graduation increase, college enrollment, and college graduation increase. We see evidence of success in all areas."

Why Do They Do What They Do?

Community educators get involved with this work for many reasons. Some have themselves come from difficult backgrounds and are "paying it forward" because they are grateful for programs or individual adult teachers and mentors who helped them overcome their own obstacles. Others, like Donyata Washington, founded programs that were not available when they were children. Washington started Virginia Kids Eat Free to provide food because "children cannot learn when they are hungry. I know because I went to school hungry."

The goal of some community educators is to stop problems before they escalate. One, who works with "at-risk youth," believes in "the power of human relationships" and the importance of "serving the community by taking action before youth are in trouble."

One characteristic that all of the community educators seem to have in common is passion—a passion to make positive changes in the lives of young people. As Kathy O'Keeffe explains, "It is the faces of those who need tools to enhance their own quality of life that motivates what I do." One survey respondent describes a "commitment to children who need a caring adult added to their current life situation to expand views of themselves and positive possibilities," while another offers a simple desire to provide a "safe and nurturing place for young people." Still another says she has a "passion to see change" and "the impact of the program on the lives of the young people."

Community educators are also passionate in their belief that young people have the potential to succeed, if only they are given the tools. One survey respondent said she has a firm "belief in the inherent value and potential of young people to contribute to their own life and the community." Another cites the "need to provide youth

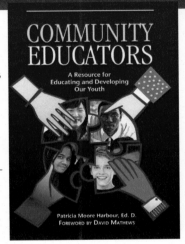

If you really want to know some ways to improve the education and development of the youth in your community, read this timely and inspiring book. Find out why, in a democracy, the public is responsible for educating its youth.

> *Antoinette Crichton Hawkins*, former elementary and high school teacher and college instructor

---

I want to congratulate Harbour on writing a much needed treatise for popular consumption on what communities are doing to help young people understand that they are cared about and that they are valuable.

> *Goldie Watkins Bryant*, former New York City Deputy Commissioner for Health

---

This book is timely and welcomed. Its emphasis on the community taking responsibility and the need for collaboration to improve education is nothing less than crucial. . . . It is . . . how we will strengthen our civilization.

> *Julie O'Mara*, former national president, American Society for Training and Development, and author

---

Community Educators is an honest account of our inability to truly transform our education system. . . . Harbour challenges us . . . to have the courage to take responsibility for our role in the education of young people.

> *Kim Eisenreich*, Senior Associate Afterschool Initiatives, Institute for Youth, Education & Families, National League of Cities

---

With up to 40 percent of American youth in many communities unable to participate productively in our society, the very future of our country depends not only upon effective transformation of our schools, but transformation of understanding that education requires engagement by entire communities.

> *Phil Stewart*, professor emeritus, The Ohio State University, and director of the Berwick Boys Foundation

---

This is an important book! Certainly, we all give lip service to the idea that it takes a village to raise a child, but this book translates this idea into concrete ways in which we all—individuals and institutions, not only schools—have important roles to play in the education of our children.

> *Diane U. Eisenberg*, president, Eisenberg Associates

Community Educators is a much needed study of developing young people's capacities beyond the school zone.

> **David W. Brown**, coeditor of Kettering's Higher Education Exchange and author of The Real Change-Makers: Why Government Is Not the Problem or the Solution

---

In *Community Educators*, Pat Harbour challenges all of us to broaden our view of youth learning and education to include "community educators" as key partners. Pat's call for collaborative relationships among citizens in all community sectors has inspired my belief that we can make a positive transformative difference in fostering the healthy development and optimal education of our children.

> **Becky Cooper**, executive director, Friends for Youth, Inc.

Through the tracing of reform efforts, research, and stories of real-life experiences, one cannot help but realize we must transform our paradigm about education. . . . Do we have the *will* to change? READ THIS BOOK!

> **Mary K. Boyd**, former area superintendent, Saint Paul, MN, Public Schools; interim dean of the Graduate School of Education, Hamline University; interim director, Services to Children and Families, Ramsey County, MN

This publication challenges all of us to reexamine our values and beliefs not only about educational achievement but about the interconnectedness between education, community, and democracy. . . . Readers are inspired to redefine our conversation about school reform to one of transforming education. As a youth-development professional, I found this publication to be a breath of fresh air. . . . I highly recommend this publication.

> **Kathryn W. Johnson**, executive director, Alternatives, Inc.

In light of the current attacks on an affordable college education we can ill afford to turn our heads and ignore what is happening with increasing regularity in our school systems. Our children are often caught up in the winds of political change with little thought of the ramifications. . . . Hat's off to "Dr. Pat" for bringing this issue to the forefront!

> **Velicia Waymer**, CPLP Training Design & Development Specialist, 1st Advantage Federal Credit Union

---

REVIEWERS RESPOND

Who among us has not wondered, fretted, puzzled, and perhaps even grieved over the seemingly intractable combination of problems impeding our collective attempts to overcome the dismal legacy of this nation in the mission of educating our youth. . . . I share Harbour's vision that the solution is within ourselves. . . . *We the People* must become *We the Educators*.

> *Capt. Rupert W. Church*, USAF (ret.); former program director, General Dynamics

This book clearly brings forth the understanding that education is more, much more than schooling. . . . It is made clear by cited experiences and examples that the education of the whole child is best achieved when the community as a whole is engaged.

> *David C. Farley*, scoutmaster, Boy Scouts of America; former community foundation executive

I think Patricia Harbour is really on to something. There is a freshness to her approach. . . . This book helps those of us in the community and in the schools to see how we are interconnected. Harbour has written a book that has created a framework for real dialogue.

> *Juan Carlos Arauz*, executive director, E3: Education, Excellence & Equity

This book is a winner. . . . The reader is guided on a meaningful journey that melds the roles of parents, teachers, community educators, action leaders, business directors, and grassroots principles into program successes, supported by a passion for fostering the success of the youth they serve.

> *Beverly Mattox*, author, former school administrator, and training specialist

Pat Harbour makes a clear distinction between "reform" and "transformation." Reform . . . is the equivalent of rearranging the furniture; this can't take us anywhere that matters. Transformation, in contrast, is systemic change. I feel confident that teachers and communities working together as partners can bring the transformation. . . . Pat Harbour, I thank you. And I assure you that you don't stand alone as you reach for transformation.

> *Bob Cornett*, "recovering" Kentucky bureaucrat and co-director Festival of the Bluegrass, Lexington, KY

with positive opportunities and outlets that help them learn how to be engaged citizens," and still another strives "to discover students' talents and help them develop them."

One respondent to the community educators survey, for example, shared this story of a young man who was able to discover and develop his talents—with profound and lasting results:

> We have in our eight years had more than one student who fits the "Max" example, but he was the first and in many ways the guiding light. I accepted this student in our first year. I liked his parents and immediately liked Max. However, he was a beaten and entirely lost student. He could not look you in the eye; he could not engage in social intercourse—his head was down, his spirit broken. Though given many opportunities, he had failed academically. He had "learning differences" and focus issues. He presented to me as defeated, diffident, apathetic, and miserable . . . but he liked to draw. Over the course of four years [working with our program], Max raised his head, learned to speak in public, became a popular student, and achieved academic success. He did this because he was allowed and encouraged to be an artist. Because he began to believe in his artistic ability, he was willing to work in other academic areas; he was willing to learn how to compensate for his learning differences.

Many community educators are motivated by the potential of an individual like Max. Others are also motivated and encouraged by the knowledge that their work has an impact that goes beyond the relatively few young people that they might work with directly. One, for example, points to an "understanding that even though this is a small program, it has the capacity to reach several thousand kids each year and provide enough encouragement and support to create hope for their future."

Several participants in the community educators research conversations spoke directly about passion, commitment, enthusiasm, and other common characteristics of the individuals and organizations engaged in this work:

> The most valuable characteristics that I found, that the most innovative community educators possessed, were vision,

passion, persistence and the ability to create meaningful and sincere connections with youth. — **Sharon Richardson**

I am committed to helping build "learning communities" for all children and youth. Finally, I will continue to work with schools to broaden their educational view to include citizen engagement in order to more effectively teach and increase the quality of life for our youth. —**Becky Cooper**

We hope that through this body of work, schools and community educators can more effectively partner in an effort to make a difference in this nation's youth. — **Stephanie Burch**

No matter its origins, people who share a passion for the next generation are recognizable to each other and to young people. — **Kathy Johnson**

Every participant had a passion for youth, which was almost palpable. . . . As each discussed their programs, their enthusiasm and energy was evident. . . . Their commitment to youth development was evident. —**Stephanie Burch**

What Changes and Impacts Have Resulted from the Programs?

Some of the impacts on young people are obvious, as when a struggling student becomes a successful one, or when a "trouble-maker" enthusiastically joins an arts program instead of a gang. Some of the impacts are more subtle, yet no less profound for the individual youth. One survey respondent, for example, wrote that "many youth in our state have experienced 'firsts' with our program, i.e. first time in a canoe, nature hike, fish caught, experience with wildlife, and many more."

Others point to impacts that contribute to a child's, and a community's, improved quality of life, or that create an environment where a child can be his or her best self: "Our impact includes creating a safe space for students to be smart (and) cultivating a community of critical thinkers that are encouraged and prepared to contribute to the communities they join. We focus on ensuring that students are well-rounded and emotionally healthy."

Another survey respondent describes a program that:

provide(s) informal education in a safe environment with adult supervision during after-school hours when parents are working. Students are not left unsupervised, so they are less likely to get involved in drugs, gangs, other juvenile offenses, and other dangers during the time after school while their parents are at work.

Another important impact of youth-development programs is that they are changing the way youth are perceived by others in their communities. Through their involvement with these programs, young people are learning to participate and contribute as citizens in many places. The programs are, in the words of Cynthia Guyton, "allowing young people to have a voice." That direct, positive involvement of young people is just one way youth-development programs are con-tributing more broadly to community development. In other words, in communities where these programs are active, youth are coming to be viewed not as a problem to be solved, but as a resource to be tapped. As George Crawley explains, his community is "using resources in the community that already exist" and "preparing all of our youth to be tomorrow's leaders."

The words of two survey respondents echo that connection be-tween community educators programs and active citizenship, and between youth development and community development:

Because (our program) works in partnership with the city . . . our work has contributed to a community culture where young people are viewed as assets and resources. Their viewpoints are sought, they are provided financial resources to oversee, and they are invested in the success of their community.

We now have youth attending meetings of the decision makers in McDowell County. Not just attending—but active participants in the meetings. We are developing our leaders of tomorrow and getting the community to see the value of collective leadership.

What Did Participants in the Community Educators Research Learn?

Participants in this research learned a great deal from one another. Some lessons learned came in the form of tangible ideas for their programs, but just as important, participants also gained insights into the fundamental importance of their work. They discussed some of these insights during research conversations, as well as informally over meals they shared together. Here are some of their comments:

> Networking and learning more about other programs helps us to build the relationships we need to have in place to collaborate and partner with each other. —**Mindy Sturm**

> My definition of "community educators" was broadened.
> —**Everett Browning**

> Participating in the community educators research conversation expanded my perception of education beyond academic environments.—**Carlenia Jackie Jackson**

> I gained an increased appreciation for collaborative work.
> —**Morrell Todd**

> Education is such a key because, as was brought out in the (research conversations), without an educated public, democracy becomes vulnerable. —**Kathy O'Keeffe**

> I learned the importance of networking. —**James Graves**

Tiffany Mitchell, a former youth participant and currently an intern with the National League of Cities, brought to one research conversation the experiences of a young person who had benefitted from a community educators program. Tiffany participated in the Alternatives, Inc. program in Hampton, Virginia. Her experience provided insight for participants as they discussed strategies, ideas, and considerations for the future of their programs. "Being a product of community education in combination with traditional schooling was vital to my success," Tiffany reported. "And," she added, "I am only at the beginning of my journey."

Looking Forward to What's Next

The energy, vibrancy, and enthusiasm with which participants left these conversations were matched only by the dedicated commitment with which they followed up with each other. In the Hampton Roads area of Virginia, some programs wrote proposals jointly, shared materials, and collaborated in other ways after experiencing the community educators research. This was an unintended benefit, as two communities in close proximity and yet separated by two bridges and two distinct lifestyles—one urban and one rural—reached out to support one another. The experience in Hampton Roads is an example of what is possible when communities, program leaders, and youth make connections to form a network to advance their mutual goals of youth education and development.

In conversations, formal and informal, community educators inspired deep reflection and projected what is valuable for the future of their community educators programs. They began to articulate what is next for them, as well as what is important to consider for a quality program.

Below, community educators continue, in their own voices, to share ideas and strategies for moving forward. Strategies and areas for consideration seem to apply most frequently to these four areas: youth development, community development, emerging concerns, relationships, and sociocultural change.

Youth Development

When community educators talked about priorities for "what's next," and for what is important for youth development in the future, most of their comments echoed several themes. It's important "to develop leadership among our youth," said one, while another pointed out that it is crucial to "recognize one's talents, capabilities, potential, and value to self, family, and community." Still another looked ahead to the value of "youths giving back," as they themselves undertake "acts of volunteering in the community."

Community Development

Repeatedly during the course of the community educators research, we found that youth development often led to broader community development. One participant noted community educators' role in "community-based research," while another pointed out "the need to connect people to resources, and resources to each other." Community educator Pam King said that programs like hers can:

> provide a network for exchange that permits our youth to meet and find out what matters relating to participating in the democratic life. . . . Meeting between our youth and decision makers seems to be a critical component. . . . This kind of forum will help develop trust among the key players and enable them to work together for the common goal and solution.

Emerging Concerns

Community educators also talked about emerging concerns, areas that needed attention in their respective communities, in order to, in one participant's words, "revitalize a community so that its residents can be healthy, happy, and proud." One participant described those emerging concerns succinctly, as a need for "cultural identity development . . . strengthening families . . . community building."

Several community educators were concerned about what one described as "rapidly changing demographics, a growing demand for a higher educated workforce, and a need for scalable solutions for public education success," and many saw "the need to create an environment within the community that embraces and promotes youth development."

While the community educators, as mentioned earlier, all shared a passion for their work, they also saw a need for greater involvement among others in the community. One called for "collective leadership to address community challenges . . . social and environmental justice," and another acknowledged that it was necessary "to increase the competencies of adults who work with youth to improve quality programs."

Relationships

We noticed that participants in research conversations and the survey repeatedly cited the value of relationships in successful and positive youth development, youth performance, and positive community development. They spoke broadly of "youth and adult partnerships," of "mentoring relationships," and of "cultural information exchanges"—and of the role those kinds of relationships can play in "academic development." Some participants focused on relationships between youth and particular people in the community: one noted the value of developing positive relationships between "public safety personnel and youth."

In the expressions quoted above, program founders, directors, and other participants give a strong indication, in their own words, of the ways in which community educators programs can be a catalyst for social and cultural change.

Sociocultural Change

Community educators programs are influencing changes in perspective, thinking, and relationships among adults and youth within the community. They are further generating change in cultural traditions, patterns of behavior, and the use of community resources. They are changing what after-school programs do, from providing babysitting and recreation services, to offering opportunities for more meaningful engagement of youth in the community.

The experiences of adults and youth working together have generated a positive influence in how they perceive and think about each other. These relationships have contributed to a change in how young people view themselves, and have led them to behave differently in their communities and schools.

Through these programs, youth have found their voices and are being heard. In many instances, young people's traditional roles and responsibilities are changing, so that rather than simply expecting to be served, youth are serving and taking responsibility for issues that concern them and their communities. For example, through a partnership between the Community Action Coalition and the Suffolk, Virginia, public schools, students are taking ownership and responsibility by providing leadership through their "Be Fight Free" campaign to end youth violence.

Contrary to an earlier way of thinking, that "children are to be seen and not heard," through many community educators programs, youth are being heard—and they are making a difference. Youth are seen as valued assets, resources, leaders, researchers, peer mentors, stakeholders, and civic activists. For instance, on the west side of Salt Lake City, Utah, youth in the Mestizo Arts and Activism project are learning, through participatory action research, how to be change agents in their community. The goal of this project is to create a shift in how the community thinks and acts as it relates to stereotypes of immigrants and discrimination against people of color in Salt Lake City. Youth in this program develop action plans to effect change in their community. (The Mestizo Arts and Activism project is discussed on pages 98–104.)

As Patrick Johnson, earlier in this book, explains in "Fostering a Culture of Youth Leadership," young people in Hampton, Virginia, have also found that their voices matter. Over time, young people in Hampton interacted and worked with elected officials, and ultimately were influential in the city council's decision to authorize and appropriate funds to build a multimillion-dollar teen center. Since its completion, the center has been operated by young people and has served teens, families, and the wider community.

Among the powerful accomplishments reported in the community educators study, programs have helped youth to develop leadership, research, and presentation skills, and, perhaps just as important, to gain self-esteem, confidence, and competence in many areas that expanded education beyond the boundaries of schooling.

Observing actions like those described above indicate that youth-leadership development is one of the ways community educators programs are building a foundation to initiate change. A shift in the way of thinking alters a mind-set that "children should only be heard" to a new way of thinking, in which youth voices are valuable—and therefore should be heard. Each program director and staff member with whom I spoke had a clear mission that focused on some dimension of youth development that was important for their community. Each seemed to actively work toward change, including change in how young people think about themselves, how adults and the community think about youth, and how they engage youth in the community. Over time, this has the potential to change the old paradigm, which so often isolates youth from their communities.

Do community educators programs illustrate a possibility for change in communities? We noticed that not only did programs challenge individual and community beliefs about who youth are and how they can benefit community, but they challenged in other ways as well. It seems the relationships and partnerships that grow out of these programs can generate a change in the focus and alignment of different sectors, allowing them to work together on behalf of youth after school.

These collaborative connections also offer a new way of behaving, or acting, as a community. We noticed that some community educators programs reported a change in the community's attitude and expectations for youth. For instance, the goal of a communitywide effort in St. Louis Park, Minnesota, "Children First," is for citizens to take ownership of youth development and education. With citizens taking responsibility for developing youth assets, young people have greater access to community resources and support for developing assets.

This focus on developing community "assets" draws from the "40 Developmental Assets" developed by the Search Institute, an organization dedicated to "discovering what kids need to succeed." The 40 Developmental Assets provides a framework for positive experiences and personal qualities that enable young people to develop into healthy, caring, and responsible citizens. Within this framework, assets fall into a number of categories that support young people to grow into their personal best. For example, under the category of "Commitment to Learning" are five assets, including "achievement motivation," which requires that a "young person is motivated to do well in school"; and "school engagement," which requires that a "young person is actively engaged in learning." Under the category of "Positive Values" are six assets: "caring," "equality and justice," "integrity," "honesty," "responsibility," and "restraint." Another category is "Social Competencies," which includes assets of "planning and decision making," "interpersonal competence," and "cultural competence."

In St. Louis Park, citizens' work on developing assets is leading to the kind of authentic change that means a shift in beliefs, attitudes, practices, and patterns for making new decisions and taking action. Rules and policies reflect the departure from "the usual" way. As new habits, structures and relationships replace or expand former interactions and patterns, individual and collective thinking, behavior, and actions change.

Results reported by participants in the community educators study seem to reveal significant sociocultural change. Evidence of this is seen in changes in relationships, as well as within individuals, youth, and adults. Changes occur in community behavior patterns, cultural customs, beliefs, roles, and responsibilities.

To examine the conditions and directions for your community, you and others might consider initiating an assessment of the social and cultural practices, habits, and patterns that impact youth. Consider the following questions along with others you may generate:

- What are the collective cultural and social customs and traditions in your community that influence our perception of and actions with youth?

- What are your individual beliefs and attitudes about youth in your community?

- Other than school, what programs or specific actions in your community currently contribute to educating and developing young people? What specifically do they do?

- How do institutional and legal practices, policies, and requirements impact youth and citizen engagement in their education and development? How are they beneficial? Or not?

- What do we want for the next generation of young people?

- Who would you talk to about this, and how would you engage others in the conversation? Who should be at the table?

Frequently, we are unaware of how our beliefs, thinking, feelings, and relationships with others influence our actions. It seems that the community educators are working to change perspectives and beliefs about youth, as well as the relationships between youth and adults. They are engaging the community to contribute its talent, expertise, and other resources to make a difference in the lives of young people.

These programs are not without problems. In fact, there are challenges and obstacles that they encounter even though many of them have operated continuously for 5, 10, 15 years, or more. As you read the next chapter, consider what challenges might confront you and your community in implementing a communitywide focus on youth education and development.

========================A STORY FROM THE FIELD========================

Youth . . . Agents of Community Change

A Case Study of the Mestizo Arts and Activism Collective*

We the People . . .We the people of the Westside
We from Your so called "shadow" lands, . . .
My home, . . . My pride Land. . . . Come one, . . .
Come all. Welcome Home, homes! . . .
We are the familia, the people.
We the familia who cares and has each other's back.
We the ones that regulate. It is obvious we will not
melt into the pot, but rather will savor our flavors in a
pico de gallo bowl. We are most importantly
the people who make up Utah.

—excerpt from spoken word piece by
West Side Youth, 2009
Mestizo Arts and Activism Collective

In *"Why Do They Hate Us?"* Caitlin Cahill describes a meeting of the 2009 Utah State legislative session, for which the Mestizo Arts and Activism Collective collaborated with the Liberation School to perform the spoken word piece "We the People." The young people who performed this powerful piece gave voice, together, to a guiding principle of our democracy. By evoking the US Constitution, "We the People," they acknowledge the inalienable right of all citizens in the United States to have an equal voice. Their poetry puts a face on social injustice and the injury

---

* This story was based on interviews with Caitlin Cahill, and written works by Caitlin Cahill, Matt Bradley, David Quijada, and C. Kinspaisby-Hill. We are deeply grateful for Cahill's permission to quote from the publications and interviews regarding the Mestizo Arts and Activism Collective and Growing Up in Salt Lake City research project. Complete references may be found in the Bibliography.

that is often incurred, both by individuals and the community, in spite of these high national ideals. These courageous young people are a part of the Mestizo Arts and Activism Collective in Salt Lake City, Utah, where young people are rising "change agents" in the community.

The Mestizo Arts and Activism (MAA) Collective is a think tank where students, researchers, artists, and mentors work collaboratively to conduct research, make changes in their community, and express themselves through the arts. MAA is a university-community partnership that involves faculty from the University of Utah, University Neighborhood Partners, and the Mestizo Institute for Culture & Arts.

On the Collective's website (mestizoactivism.blogspot.com), MAA youth describe themselves as "an intergenerational group of students of diverse academic and ethnic backgrounds concerned about the community we live in," and as "poets, painters, graffiti artists, musicians, dancers, activists, student leaders, high school and university students, community organizers, and researchers who work collaboratively." Why do they do what they do? They explain: "We use our research and personal experiences as a way of promoting social justice and of making our voices heard. We are inspired and motivated to create positive change by understanding and addressing the issues our communities face daily."

Young people who participate in Mestizo Arts and Activism use the arts as a tool for learning, developing leadership skills, and engaging in research. They contribute to raising awareness of social issues through their performances, video presentations, and other forms of art and community dialogue. In several cities in Utah, for example, MAA participants have led intercultural dialogues, with positive results reported among citizen participants. Youth have shared powerful stories of their experiences and have found meaning in the face of the most negative and difficult circumstances.

The Mestizo Arts and Activism Collective uses participatory action research (PAR), a collaborative approach to research and education, as a way for youth to explore often-complicated social issues. Central to this approach is the specific action that follows the research; in other words, it is not just theoretical, but practical.

For example, in "Participatory Praxis and Social Justice," Mestizo codirector Cahill describes what happened a few years ago, when a 16-year-old Latino boy named Esteban Saidi was shot and killed by another teenager, a Pacific Islander, in Salt Lake City. The tragedy was said to be in retribution for an earlier stabbing, and, through their response, local media and law enforcement officials inadvertently fanned the flames of racial tension.

Several of the young people on the MAA research team knew Esteban very well. As a group of them read a newspaper account of the killing, their response was heartfelt: "What! This is not the Esteban I knew! This is not Esteban!!!" One friend, Lily, was very upset. "How could they say this about him? Can't they let him die peacefully? . . . They don't even know him." Lily went to church camp with him. Another young man, Jorge, lived a block away from Esteban and played with him as a child. A few went to school with him, remembering him as the quiet boy who often sat in the back of the classroom.

These young people might have reacted in anger, further fueling a community's rage. But in the Mestizo Arts and Activism Collective, youth learn how to allow such events to motivate them to take positive action, and to awaken a new consciousness and awareness within themselves and their community.

As the students worked through their grief over Esteban's death, they seemed to access an even deeper loss. Esteban's death fueled grieving of not only the loss of a friend, but a loss of who he was. They were truly shocked and hurt reading how the media described Esteban in their report of this tragedy. It seemed Esteban's friends suffered a loss of his identity, and in some ways, their own. This misrepresentation of Esteban reflected on who they were as well.

The young people reported that the reaction to the tragedy by institutions—media, school district, local school, and police—seemed to escalate beyond the incident and negatively characterized youth in the Latino community. For them, it was true that Esteban, a Latino, was killed by Ricky Angilau, a Pacific Islander, but Esteban was not a troublemaker or gang member, nor did he fit the other negative stereotypes with which he had been labeled. The students felt that a lock-down imposed by their school principal, the intense police surveillance of Esteban's neighborhood, and increased instances of racial profiling in the community were heavy-handed and unnecessary. The more they read and observed official reactions to the stabbing, the more they began to believe that labeling and stereotyping were the lens through which reaction, actions, and decisions were being made. Yet instead of responding impulsively, this is what they did:

> Together we processed the shock, the loss, and the wider social impacts of his death. We created a space for grieving collectively. And, beyond this, we spent time talking and thinking through the roots of racial divisions within our communities and ways to bring people together. We began a participatory action research project.

The youth in the Mestizo Arts and Activism Collective recognized that labeling and stereotyping is damaging, not only to those targeted but also to those who label others, and to members of the community-at-large. They identified their findings as "institutional racism," and used them as motivation for a research project they called: "LABELED: Telling Our Own Story." The project focuses on how the media and other institutions often misrepresent youth of color. Through this project and others, youth in the Mestizo Arts and Activism Collective have been a catalyst for change, specifically regarding social justice and discrimination.

In "Documenting (In)Justice: Community-Based Participatory Research and Video," Caitlin Cahill and Matt Bradley describe *Red Flags: Stereotyping & Racism in the Schools*, a video produced as part of Growing Up in Salt Lake City, a collaborative participatory action research project, which focused on young people and the social injustices they faced in school. The young people in the project found that stereotyping and racism can be a major challenge to their success in school and can threaten their sense of identity, community relationships, and equity for all citizens. In the words of Kanesha, one *Red Flags* high school researcher who worked on a video as part of the participatory research project:

> Racism is a big part of daily life in school. We decided to make our documentary on stereotyping and racism in school because we all experienced it in school. That is a huge part of our life and it's a huge problem in schools and it's really hard to deal with sometimes. As I look back on when we were in the documentary process, the things that stood out more to me were knowing that teenagers my age are going through the same things in school as me. They all want what we want: to let people see that racism has not stopped—it is still here—and also let the adults know how it's affecting us, changes how we perform in school, and even makes us not want to go any more. Another thing that stands out was hearing from the people we interviewed their personal stories, because I could relate to it and say, "Hey, I am not the only one going through this!!"

The prevalence of institutional racism—often unconscious behaviors, policies, rules, or particular ways of thinking—was one of the primary themes that emerged from the *Red Flags* research. Institutional racism is especially detrimental because it is prejudice that has become so ingrained that its patterns and practices may be no longer noticeable. The actions of certain individuals or groups, and ways of communicating with or about "the other" are often unintentional and diminish all who are involved. The Growing Up in Salt Lake City research team wanted to increase awareness of institutional racism communitywide, recognizing that only through increased awareness and conscious choice can the community individually and collectively choose to change behaviors. It is in that moment of choice that change can occur.

The Growing Up in Salt Lake City team chose to produce a video in order to make their message available to audiences who may not traditionally be involved in research. Through the video they hoped to reach and to educate other teenagers of color. They also hoped to educate teachers and administrators, by examining both stereotyping and racism.

Kanesha's brave decision to share her story publically in the video inspired the whole research team and became a turning point for their research. In the video, rather than simply telling her story, she dramatized her experience with a principal who had accused her of bringing a knife to school. After repeatedly explaining that she had not brought a knife to school, Kanesha reported being aggressively questioned, and made to empty her pockets. She was wearing her hair pinned up. The principal made her take her hair down to demonstrate she did not have a knife. In the video, it is clear that Kanesha's hair could not hide a knife.

Others also presented compelling scenes to convey their own experiences with institutional racism. One young man, Joel, whose family speaks Spanish, dramatized his experience of being made to take the ESL test every year, even though he speaks fluent English and takes an Advanced Placement English class at school. A young woman named Naima staged her experience with students who laughed at her in the school hallway for wearing a hijab, the traditional head covering worn by some Muslim women and young girls.

Some of the stories of discrimination were painful for the young people to share. Some had not shared them with anyone else before. Yet the team hoped that when others witnessed their stories of intimate humiliation, they might empathize and be stretched beyond their comfort zones. The video might allow a viewer to consider another person's experiences, feelings, and thoughts about the impact of institutional racism and prejudice.

One of the main goals of using video reenactments, rather than simple storytelling, according to Cahill and Bradley, was "to inspire others to be brave enough to reflect upon their own experiences of racism and stereotyping, to start a conversation about these threatening subjects, and find the courage to speak back in public."

The young people engaged in the Mestizo Arts and Activism Collective have reached out to other groups to share their experiences and inspire other youth to find their voices and contribute to change in their communities. One group that has used the *Red Flags* video is Youth in Focus of Oakland, California. Project coordinator Aaron Nakai, explained her reason for using the video: "Steel sharpens steel, and young folks are pushed further and hold themselves to higher standards when they see the strong work of other youth around the country and world."

CHAPTER FOUR

CHALLENGES AND OBSTACLES

Past school reforms that gave lip service to public participation have left what researchers describe as a legacy of distrust. The ever-increasing bureaucratization of schools has resulted in ever-increasing frustration for both teachers and citizens. Defensive, hands-off professionalism (claiming that the classroom is like an operating room) alienates would-be allies in the community.

David Mathews, Reclaiming Public Education by Reclaiming Our Democracy

In the community educators research, participants examined the challenges and obstacles they faced in their programs and communities. During the research conversations we examined these issues through the lens of a series of questions which included the following:

- With what challenges do communities struggle?
- What obstacles do they face as they attempt to meet those challenges?
- How do they overcome these obstacles to move forward their youth-development efforts?

As they addressed these questions, community educators in the research conversations identified a number of challenges. By definition, their programs all grew in one way or another out of challenges relating to youth in communities; their primary missions responded to specific concerns about youth. On the other hand, the obstacles these educators faced while meeting those challenges varied; nevertheless, both the research conversations and the Community Educators Survey revealed six obstacles the respondents reported most frequently: insufficient access to reliable funding; understaffing; red tape and bureaucratic obstacles in schools; a scarcity of available, qualified mentors; the challenge of attracting youth and enabling their participation; and a scarcity of appropriate space/facilities.

Funding

Not surprisingly, funding was the biggest obstacle to program implementation and sustainability, with 87 percent of survey respondents identifying it as such. Although most of the programs have been able to obtain some level of funding, they still face difficulties in maintaining an adequate degree of financial support. As a result, program leaders spend a significant amount of time "helping funders and systems understand the comprehensive nature of our work and what children and families need." Yet the problem is not simply a scarcity of funds at any given time, but also the difficulty of maintaining a reliable, steady funding stream, or "access to adequate funding year to year," in the words of one survey respondent. Given that both research conversation participants and survey respondents mentioned grants as the primary source of funding (followed by private donors, community sponsors, and businesses), the programs are often at the mercy of the grant cycle, making it necessary to spend a substantial amount of time and resources just to keep the program afloat.

One community group that struggled with financial issues—and still had a significant positive impact—was in Albion, Michigan. Community educators from that Midwestern city described how their local communitywide education initiative began. Youth development had become a local priority as various concerns about youth and their relationship to the community mounted. The concerns grew as youth violence, vandalism, low school performance, teen pregnancy, and high school dropout rates increased. From a different perspective, many people were concerned about the high number of local youth who moved away from the community and did not return to live there.

Schools were included as a part of the efforts to address these concerns; however, as a community-initiated endeavor, community leaders and a paid executive director provided leadership and coordination for the volunteers, programs, and events scheduled for youth. Local businesses, foundations, and private donors gave initial funds for the ongoing undertaking. Citizens from all walks of life were encouraged to participate, and they volunteered in a multitude of ways to make a difference in the lives of their community's young people. They tutored, mentored, offered special courses, and served as a support system, all of which created substantial synergy and unity throughout the community. Historical, social, cultural, racial, and economic boundaries seemed to disappear as individuals and organizations formed new and deeper relationships. Ultimately, a focus on youth development fostered increased collaboration, which led in turn to community development.

Yet in spite of its notable positive impact on the community, the program as such no longer exists in Albion. Although the community recognized itself as a resource, and everyone had something important to contribute, insufficient funds prevented the communitywide effort from continuing. Eventually, through a domino effect, the program seemed to tumble and fall. The loss of funds supporting the program led to the elimination of the coordinator's position. Changes in leadership as the founders retired or relocated from the city also impacted this communitywide effort for youth development. Still, nearly every person I interviewed in that community showed incredible commitment and a sense of ownership. In spite of the obstacles and challenges that ultimately ended the program, they made it clear that their commitment was not to programs but to youth.

Because of this kind of commitment, one community activist and leader continues to build collaborative partnerships on behalf of young people in Albion. He told me he had learned that funding was not the most important element; rather, collaboration, commitment, and shared resources ultimately mattered much more. Another founding leader shared with me that although they may have lost the larger coordinated program, he believed that what they gained was far greater: they gained a community that matured in its development while working together on behalf of youth. He also noted that the community had gained citizens who individually and collectively are willing to col-

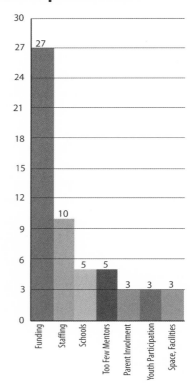

Challenges to Program Implementation

Number of Coding References

Funding · 27
Staffing · 10
Schools · 5
Too Few Mentors · 5
Parent Involvment · 3
Youth Participation · 3
Space, Facilities · 3

Node:

As shown in the graph above, survey respondents reported a number of obstacles to their work. Participants in the research conversations devoted a significant amount of time and passion to discussing them as well.

laborate on behalf of young people, and still do. The spirit of many in this community is demonstrated by their continued efforts to initiate and maintain a focus on the development of youth, even though the structure and the form may be different today from what it was just a few years ago. In many ways this community is both recovering and attempting to overcome the obstacles and challenges it has faced.

Relationship to Schools

Several community educators pointed out that access to their local school districts is often difficult, largely because of district policies and bureaucratic mazes that restrict communication and collaboration. Survey respondents also reported that the lack of access to schools can minimize citizens' perception of how they can contribute to the education and development of youth in their communities. They reason, "If schools are the place where kids are educated, and we are unable to access the schools, then we will be unable to help educate our kids."

Lack of access is not the whole story of the relationship between community educators programs and schools, however. Data from the overall study suggest a dichotomous relationship between these programs and their local schools. While respondents often reported that schools present obstacles that preclude working together, many also strongly asserted that schools are necessary and essential to their programs. In every case, participants in the research conversations said they valued the schools and the opportunity to work with them. In fact, two of the programs were located in school buildings. One Maryland program, funded by a joint grant with the school district, held its after-school program in a school facility and employed teachers as tutors.

Still, the path to achieving such collaboration can be difficult, and the Kettering Foundation has observed for many years the tendency of schools to keep the community at arms' length. An unpublished Kettering Foundation study called "Community-School Bonding," based on research undertaken in the 1980s, examined the relationship between community members and the local school in rural Lochapoka, Alabama. Conducted as a research exchange with the Truman Pierce Institute at Auburn University's College of Education, the study looked at what it takes for schools and communities to bond and increase the opportunities for parents and other citizens to contribute to the education and development of young people.

As part of this study, I conducted several community-school workshops that brought parents, citizens, community leaders, teachers, and local and district administrators together for a series of "bonding sessions," including one overnight retreat in Eufaula, Alabama. Louise White, a well-known trainer formerly with the District of Columbia Public Schools, joined me to offer experiential learning to build school-community relationships, deliberate local issues, identify mutual values for youth education and development, and establish an agenda for working together. The retreat experience was also an opportunity for community members, parents, and school personnel to create an authentic working relationship. Throughout these sessions, and later, as we received written feedback from participants, there was every indication that we achieved the expected outcome. In practice, however, the school and the community remained distant and disconnected from one another. The image that comes to my mind is of the school administrator, with arms and legs straddling the doorway, blocking entry, as communications from the school conveyed the message: "We are the experts . . . please let us do our job."

The situation, however, was not simply a matter of arrogance on the part of school administrators. Educators in this rural Alabama district were facing pressure from the national "back to basics" movement, as were many schools in the 1980s. Making matters worse, the school community had been torn apart by a hard-fought battle to desegregate, resulting in the consolidation of many schools into a single facility, grades 8-12. Most students rode a bus two or more hours to and from school each day, and many teachers lived in other communities, a considerable distance from the school. As a result, sports teams and other after-school activities—not to mention a viable Parent Teacher Association (PTA) or Parent Teacher Organization (PTO)—were out of the question. In effect, the restructured district created a school without a community.

Nevertheless, in spite of distance and transportation difficulties, a nearby university and many community leaders, including the editor of the local newspaper, wanted to collaborate. All of them were committed to providing local support, staff development, and assistance aimed at improving the students' education. Unfortunately, the school's administrators seemed to perceive the involvement of the community and the university as an intrusion.

From the principal's perspective, community involvement was not a priority; as he saw it, additional funding for local school efforts would be of much greater benefit. Further, it seemed that the principal felt that he was under considerable scrutiny from the district's administrators. It was clear that this political relationship took precedence over other relationships. As researchers at the time, we concluded that the principal stood in the doorway to limit or prevent community engagement, and yet, looking back, I wonder whether his behavior was simply influenced by the times and local circumstances. Perhaps, for him, it was a matter of survival. Either way, neither change, reform, nor transformation occurred. Was it even possible?

Some 25 years later, KF researchers have learned that citizens in many communities find a way to contribute meaningfully to young people's education and development through after-school programs. The programs emerge when citizens shift their focus from schools as the only way to reach young people, to a broader focus on youth development rather than education. In that way, organizations and individuals have found that they can make a difference in young people's lives and well-being outside of the formal academic setting. A side benefit is that the programs' broader emphasis on youth development ultimately provides a foundation for successful academic performance, citizenship, and engagement in the community. As a result, it seems, tensions between schools and community educators often show signs of lessening.

Participants in the community educators research revealed that creating partnerships in schools is still a challenge, usually because red tape can be difficult to cut through. For example, one participant, Donyata Washington, founded an innovative program called Virginia Kids Eat Free, which provides food for children by collaborating with multiple local organizations, as well as state and federal government programs. Throughout the Hampton Roads area of Virginia, the collaborative has enabled children to eat at no cost to parents or to host organizations like the YMCA/YWCA, Boys & Girls Clubs, or faith-based groups. By partnering with these organizations and then providing meals for the children enrolled in day care, summer camps, sports teams, and other activities, Virginia Kids Eat Free can fulfill its ingeniously narrow mission—providing meals—with an enormously broad and considerable impact. As founder and program director, Washington pointed out during one research conversation that football coaches have told her that kids come to practice on time when they know that meals will be served. In fact, she continued, "Everybody across the board . . . has said that the food that we serve has increased the attendance, and the kids act better."

Initially, Virginia Kids Eat Free operated only during the summer months, meeting in churches and other locations throughout different communities. Once the year-round program was up and running, however, Donyata Washington enthusiastically attempted to partner with a local school district. About that experience, she tells a provocative story about how difficult it was to navigate through the red tape and bureaucracy in the school system. She reports that initially she felt blocked in every possible way to provide "food free" for students at the school. As she fought through the red tape, Washington stayed focused on her mission: "How do we re-frame this conversation so that everything that I have to offer, whatever talent or resources I have to offer, get used up for these kids in these schools?" Ultimately she prevailed, and the program was able to collaborate with the local schools.

Staffing, Volunteers, and Mentoring

Community educators point to a well-trained workforce as one key to ensuring quality youth-development programs. Unfortunately, staffing problems were the second-most-frequently reported obstacle to program success (next to funding difficulties). Several respondents specifically noted insufficient numbers of available staff, as well as scheduling conflicts among staff and the young people in the programs. Scheduling is an especially difficult issue for those programs that rely on volunteers, who also have commitments to employers, family, community, and other organizations.

Staffing issues did not come up as often in the research conversations as they did in the Community Educators Survey. Participants did, however, discuss the need for professional youth-development workers. In some instances participants identified recruiting and maintaining a volunteer workforce as a challenge, as it is difficult for most volunteers to make a long-term commitment, month after month, year after year. And, because business people, other professionals, and college students often volunteer as mentors and role models, having an adequate number of mentors available on a consistent schedule presents a special challenge. Sometimes a youth's mentor might be unavailable at a scheduled time, making it necessary for more than one child to share a mentor. Given that one of the key benefits of a mentoring program is the sustained, one-on-one time it gives young people with a caring adult, such an arrangement is less than ideal.

Needless to say, staffing problems often overlap with funding problems. In the Maryland program mentioned previously, a paid staff relied on assistance from community volunteers, as well as professional teachers who received a stipend to provide tutoring in an after-school program. The program had collaborated with the school and the school district to secure a grant to cover the teachers' stipend, but as the economy worsened and districts were cutting school budgets, both staffing and funding became an issue.

Limited Institutional Support

Survey respondents and research conversation participants both cited limited institutional support as a challenge. Although several of the programs collaborated to varying degrees with local government agencies or departments, schools, or other organizations, none of them was a regular, permanent part of any institution. As a result, program leaders reported that they constantly faced problems, such as insufficient office or program space, a precarious connection to funding sources, and dependence on a burnout-prone volunteer staff.

Furthermore, the competing agendas of school district personnel, along with frequent changes in school leadership, meant that a program could go in and out of favor from year to year, with a resulting increase or decrease in funds, staffing, and space.

Several program founders mentioned using their personal funds to keep programs operating, due to an absence of institutional funds. As one participant in a research conversation succinctly explained: "We have no funding, . . . we have limited institutional support, and most of it is carved out through our own resources." Such a situation is seldom sustainable.

A youth-leadership program in one Southern community, for example, grew out of local communitywide meetings on youth violence issues, but was unable to maintain consistent institutional support. A classroom teacher who lives in the community founded the program, and in a telephone interview, she told me how it began: "I stood up one night after attending several of these community meetings and declared, 'I am tired of us talking about it over and over again; somebody needs to do something.'" As soon as she said it, she recalls, she recognized that she was that somebody, so she told the group, "I will organize a leadership program for girls and boys." She left the meeting, and true to her word, this teacher and one of her colleagues launched an after-school leadership program for local youth. In the program's first year, the public recreation department provided space and a small financial contribution, but when the department's budget was cut the following year, funds were no longer available. Without a reliable funding source, the program struggled for the next two years, but the founder carried on. She provided personal funds, space, and resources to keep the program operating. Ultimately, however, she could not continue to bear this substantial financial burden, not to mention the bureaucratic red tape the program required her to deal with. As a result, I understand this leadership development opportunity for young people came to an abrupt end.

Systemic Issues

Participants in the community educators research noted several systemic issues that impeded the relationship between schools and the broader community, including ever-increasing demands for students to pass high-stakes standardized tests. In virtually every public school in the country, the curriculum has narrowed, primarily in response to testing requirements. In several research conversations, community educators discussed these high-stakes tests as a major obstacle for citizens and parents who would like to contribute meaningfully to youth in public schools.

The result of such testing requirements is a curriculum that leaves no room for the kinds of enriching experiences that the public might bring to the classroom. Parents and other individuals, as well as local businesses and civic, social, and arts organizations; all may have resources and talents to contribute. Yet if those resources and talents fall outside the scope of state testing standards, then schools simply have no time for them. It's no wonder community educators feel a declining trust in their local schools.

These tests affect virtually everyone in a school system. Graduation from high school is dependent on a student's passing; classroom teachers are assessed on the level of their students' performance on the tests; and principals are assessed by the school's overall performance. In some cases, a low-performing class or school can cause a principal or teachers to lose their jobs—a high-pressure situation that some educators have taken desperate and illegal measures to avoid.

For example, in a Roanoke, Virginia, high school in 2009, an administrator and several school personnel were accused of inaccurately reporting the scores of all the children on the state's Standards of Learning (SOL) achievement exam. According to media reports, they pulled out the exams of students whose low scores would have affected the academic standing of the school. After losing a highly publicized legal case, the principal was fired and the accused school counselors were reprimanded, demoted, and reassigned. More and more, in the eyes of the public, schools lose their credibility, and unfortunately, the integrity of educators is questioned because of the actions of a few.

Another recent cheating scandal was more widespread, involving nearly half of the public schools in Atlanta, Georgia. More than 178 principals and teachers, along with the superintendent and her staff, were accused of test fraud. Such cheating scandals seem to be on the rise. The question is, what is the cause and the cost? Some say it's the pressure that began with the demands of the No Child Left Behind Act; others claim that superintendents are setting unrealistic goals for scores on these tests, and that pressure works its way down to the principals who likewise pressure the classroom teachers. Have we created a culture of fear and pressure that opens the door to dishonesty and a lack of integrity among those who are responsible for educating the next generation of leaders in the United States of America? How does this further alienate the public from its schools?

The specter of cheating hangs over a number of school districts, and I am deeply saddened every time I read about such unconscionable actions. These reprehensible deeds tarnish not only the reputation of the actor, but the field of education. When these revered role models act with such indiscretion, the young people who believe in them and trust them are marred and are themselves vulnerable to making unwise choices.

Another systemic obstacle that community educators noted is the structure and bureaucracy through which decisions are made about everything from curriculum to staffing to funding. More often than not, they said, decisions are made by individuals and organizations with little or no real knowledge of or familiarity with schools and the young people in them.

Although it was not specifically discussed in the community educators research conversations, recent events in Newark, New Jersey, provide a useful illustration of this kind of systemic obstacle. In 2010, Newark was the recipient of a $100 million gift from Facebook founder and CEO, Mark Zuckerberg. These funds were to be matched by the city, and managed and dispersed by the Foundation for Newark's Future. The purpose of these funds was to help Newark's troubled school district, but the funding was granted with the expectation that a broad spectrum of community engagement would be the basis for determining how the funds would be used. More than 45,000 community members were contacted and approximately 36 community and "mini" forums were convened for citizens to meet and collectively discuss how the funds would be used. Unfortunately, the wind was soon knocked out of their sails.

In spite of the efforts to garner citizen input, journalist Joan Whitlow of the Newark *Star-Ledger* described how red tape and institutional practices at the Foundation for Newark's Future has precluded community involvement and diminished citizen power over decision making ("It's Facebook Money and Newark's Future," October 7, 2011). Also writing for the *Star-Ledger*, Cindy Gibson quoted the foundation's president and CEO, Gregory Taylor, as saying, "Letting the people have their say is not how professional philanthropy works" ("Newark Parents Pushed out of Decision Making on Zuckerberg Donation," October 10, 2011). Taylor explained, "The decision makers will be an advisory board to the foundation"—with one requirement for a seat on this board being a $10 million donation! Although Mayor Cory Booker had informed the community that Newark citizens would make the decisions, those hopes and expectations were immediately dashed when Taylor reportedly said that people had taken that promise too literally. So far Booker is the only advisory board member from Newark, but as Whitlow, of the *Star-Ledger*, points out, "If the goal is to improve education in Newark, the board should be expanded to include voting members from and of Newark, with a direct say in how the money is spent. That fund needs people who have a sense of what has worked and already failed, people who have a stake in the outcome."

Philanthropic organizations can be very powerful institutions in a community. The Foundation for Newark's Future provides an unfortunate example of a community institution that is not in alignment with the intent of a grant, in which citizens are engaged in how the funds should be used. The mayor, who advocated for community involvement and had been highly influential in the city's receiving the Facebook grant in the first place, was naturally concerned about the promise he made.

Unfortunately, turmoil in Newark's education system is not new. In 1997, education researcher Jean Anyon published *Ghetto Schooling: A Political Economy of Urban Educational Reform*, a personal documentation of a four-year school-reform project in Newark's public school district. Anyon's book captures how government and business policies have negatively affected the economic, political, and human resources in the community. Her book points out that education reform is unlikely without systemic change in public policy and a redirection of resources to the community and their schools. A decade and a half later, the question of who makes decisions on Mark Zuckerberg's $100 million gift is an example of how institutional practices continue to silence the voices of the public in public education.

> How would you describe and explain the relationship between various sectors in your community and the schools? What supports or is a barrier to trust, credibility, transparency, and communication? To what extent are schools, parents, and citizens connected or isolated?

Fragmentation in the Community

Some community educators reported fragmentation in the community as an obstacle to achieving as much as they would like to achieve. When different groups in the community don't know each other and are unaccustomed to working with each other, the result can be duplicated efforts and inefficient use of resources. Sometimes such fragmentation is simply a matter of people being unaware of each other; when they do become aware, they quickly learn to collaborate. That was the case in the Hampton Roads area of Virginia, where several organizations were working independently on youth issues—until representatives of these groups met each other at a community educators research conversation and soon began to collaborate. Other times, it may simply be a matter of habit, as different organizations are accustomed to working independently. Still other times, fragmentation within a community can become a problem when turf issues and limited resources are involved.

That kind of fragmentation may have contributed to some of the problems encountered by Virginia Kids Eat Free. Although that organization was able to establish a successful collaboration with public schools, as described earlier, director Donyata Washington eventually found the program caught in a political hornet's nest of other territorial and funding issues. This "political food fight" escalated to the levels of state and federal governments, both of which were providing resources and support to Virginia Kids Eat Free, as well as to other programs that provided food for children.

I wonder whether the problem was that, because of competition over those government resources, other programs wanted to shut Washington's program down. In any case, that did not happen. Instead, rather than eliminating the program, the state assigned a limited jurisdiction where Virginia Kids Eat Free could operate and continue to provide food for children. Donyata Washington's program continues to operate now and enjoys local, state, and federal support.

Sometimes community educators have to get creative to overcome the obstacles presented by a fragmented community, and those in the community educators study described a number of strategies they employed to launch their youth-development programs.

Conventional wisdom would suggest that having community support in place would be one key to implementing a successful youth-development program. Yet gathering such support can be a daunting task in fragmented communities, in which the varying sectors often have little experience working together.

One program founder, for example, faced difficulties in bringing together community members and school personnel to collaborate on a vision for an after-school program. Frustrated with local schools and the community, and unable to get the two groups to agree, she took an "if we build it, they will come" approach. That is, program leaders decided to move ahead with implementing the program and to try engaging schools and community members later. It was a risky approach, but in this case, it worked. Once the program was operating, the founder and volunteer staff invited parents, school personnel, elected officials, and other community stakeholders for a grand opening to launch the program. People in the community were impressed and began to offer their support. A local church provided funds, space, volunteers, and performing artists, such as African drummers and dancers. This program, Cultural Arts for Education, recognizes the importance of cultural identity in youth development. Teachers, along with parents, church members, and others in the community, volunteer as tutors and mentors and collaborate to ensure the future of what has become an important resource for their youth.

Still, the fully engaged community tends to be the exception rather than the rule. I wonder whether such a situation, in which community educators are repeatedly unable to garner support, suggests that the community does not recognize itself as a resource. Are community members unable to imagine the human and other resources they already possess that could help to meet the needs of their young people?

It was clear from our research that the kinds of community educators programs we studied often struggle with both funding and human resources. A great majority of these mission-driven organizations are based on the vision of an individual founder who is passionate about transforming circumstances to enable youth to improve their lives and their futures. Not surprisingly, stand-alone programs without reliable institutional or organizational affiliation generally struggle more than those that are rooted in the community, usually through a local organization, institution, and those associated with their local government.

> *Can you cite examples from your own experience that indicate that members of your community do (or do not) see themselves and their community as a valuable resource for educating and developing youth?*

I wonder how it would be for young people if a culture of learning was central to their community's thinking, mind-set, and actions? How would we describe the results where citizens, professional educators, and all sectors collaborated to ensure that educating and developing youth is a local priority? I strongly suspect this is the profile of a community that recognizes the role of the public and demonstrates ownership by taking responsibility for public education.

The findings from our data were not conclusive regarding the ways organizations overcame these obstacles, or how frequently entire communities made collective decisions as they moved forward to address the needs of their young people.

Dissatisfaction with the School-Community Relationship

In the ideal democracy, the public makes decisions about the education of its next generation of citizens. Yet given the fragmentation of communities and the often-negative public perception of education and schooling, what is clearly required is a change in habits of the mind. What is required, in other words, is a shift in the mindsets of those both inside and outside the school walls. To paraphrase David Mathews, the public must reclaim public education.

In Mathews' book, *Reclaiming Public Education by Reclaiming Our Democracy*, he acknowledges that dissatisfaction with the relationship between professional educators and citizens is mutual.

> Despite frustrations on both sides of the divide between the public and the public schools, I am convinced that enough political will could be generated to bridge the gap. Citizens don't want to sit on the sidelines of public education. I accept the findings that Americans are eager to work with educators but want a relationship among equals. Using an analogy from business, a woman from Massachusetts explained: "It's just like in a lot of industries. Where I work we're in what they call the team concept and our business is running much better than it ever did when we had a hierarchy." A man in Maryland made a similar point: "If we let the grassroots do more work I think we'd be in good shape."

> Wary educators don't always warm to such assistance because they fear citizens will invade their turf. An irate parent or special-interest group might well try to step over the line. But professionals need not be so wary. . . . The citizenry as a whole doesn't want to take over running the schools. A study of parents, who might be the most likely to want to micro-manage the schools, found that they aren't power hungry. Few want to take over administrative responsibilities or teach math. A group of citizens in West Virginia went further in

distinguishing the role of professionals from their own role. Even though mindful of the expertise teachers bring to the classroom, they were reluctant to "leave it to the professionals" to make every decision about education. These West Virginians thought that a community's collective judgment was better on some issues. Treating education as a purely professional matter, they said, "widens the gulf between the public and its schools."

All of the community educators programs in this study were initiated out of a need to which citizens and organizations could, and wanted to, respond. The challenges that they face are not isolated from the challenges of schooling, because those challenges also impact the community as a whole. Yet each community's unique culture, traditions, and history present a unique set of relationships and challenges, so that there is no one way to respond to them. Following are some questions to consider as you think about the challenges facing your community:

- How can schools and communities be supported and encouraged to find common ground with one another?
- In relationship to education, with what is your community struggling?
- With what obstacles is your community challenged? How does your community resolve these challenges and obstacles to move education forward?

People in each community must examine themselves and plan for the challenges that face youth in their distinct community. While the experiences of one community may generate ideas for the next to consider, the ultimate strategy is for citizens to make plans that meet the needs and requirements of their own community.

The Value of Steady, Committed Community Support

Ann Stiles

May is the season for high school and college graduations. Attending these events is my business. I lead a college access program that includes the satisfying task of awarding college scholarships. The students we serve live in communities historically underserved and underrepresented in higher education. We work to correct that.

I recently opened an invitation that struck a particularly resonant chord. It was from Miguel. I got to know Miguel as he was preparing to graduate from high school. He was earning our scholarship, among many others. He was the first in his family to graduate high school, but far more impressive, he was on his way to Cornell University in Ithaca, New York.

I learned much about Miguel's life through his response to the world he encountered in New York. After moving into the dorm he called to report what, to him, was the singular event so far. He had his own bed. When he was in high school, he had moved from one relative's home to another, where his bedroom was the available sofa. Both his extended family and his community had provided examples of endurance and nurturing for him, even though other aspects of his world were more variable. As a partner to his community, I know that our work helped to sustain and develop his educational aspirations. We added resources that enabled Miguel to connect his aspirations to higher education.

Miguel was soon overwhelmed by the demands of an Ivy League environment, however, and he transferred back to Houston, where he began taking classes at a local community college while also working full time. After eight years he has completed his bachelor's degree in business administration.

To me, Miguel represents the success of young adults beyond our usual measures and understanding. By many current standards, Miguel's success would be counted as failure. He did not graduate from college within the usual time allotted; he did not complete the Ivy League education offered to him. And yet, on a Saturday in May he received his bachelor's degree. He is fully employed in the information technology sector, his field of choice. Future generations in his family will point to his success as a marker for their own life journeys.

While we have been waiting on "superman" and tracking the latest innovation in school reform, debating which children were left behind and why, Miguel was steadily moving toward his goal, with the support of a community organization focused consistently on his success. Miguel was supported not by the latest technique or grandly named program but by resources more constant and steadfast.

New school leaders often arrive in a fanfare of challenge to the status quo, sometimes oblivious to what that status quo is. Suddenly, every existing effort is labeled ineffective, and the new leaders believe transformation can only be achieved when everything that went before has been swept away.

We should be impatient for all of our children to have access to the opportunities made possible by a quality education. We should expect this, and tolerate nothing less. Yet the existing landscape must not be carelessly assessed. In its haste to establish new strength and urgency, a new administration can easily miss the vital resources at work within a community.

Understanding the education of our youth only through the lens of change, innovation, and new beginnings allows education professionals to turn a blind eye to that which is constant and ever present. Communities can't be swept into the dust bin along with what remains of our "failed public school system." Communities—rich with experience, wisdom, and vested interest—are comprised of businesses in need of an educated workforce, families desperately seeking better for their children, and partners committed not to the numbers but to the children. Such a community was there for Miguel: he was hired by a local business; his family looks to him as a beacon of success; and, judging by the handwritten invitation to his graduation that we received, our organization was there for him as well. We have been there year after year, principal after principal, superintendent after superintendent.

This is the American story, a story passed from generation to generation. The community was here before the latest wave of reform and will be here long after. The community's vision is for the long-term, not for the term of office. The quick turnaround sought by an ever less patient electorate is an illusion. Today's quick turnaround is tomorrow's legacy of failure.

From the stories of families, I have learned the greater value of the scholarships we provide in creating possibilities and shaping dreams. I know the importance of our constancy within communities in order to sustain a vision that is about more than passing tests and more than high school graduation. When I received Miguel's invitation, I looked back at his academic record in our system. Each semester he sent us his transcript. Each semester, even after his four years of scholarship funding was concluded, he let us know where he was taking classes, his hours completed, his grade-point average. His recorded progress, the evidence of his checking in over these eight years, has provided me with the proof of constancy I have sought. As schools are whipsawed from one point of light to another, from this magic bullet to that, it is the community that will care for its own. Miguel's lived story of success has been supported by a rich collection of resources over time, from the sofas of extended family members, a scholarship offer, and ongoing encouragement to persist. The community endures. This is the community I choose to be a part of.

Ann B. Stiles, EdD,— is executive director of Project GRAD in Houston, Texas. Her work is focused on community-based collaborations to improve the college readiness, access, and success for historically underserved and underrepresented students, Hispanic and African American students from low-income communities and students who are among the first-generation in their families to enroll in higher education. Stiles began her career in education as a teacher in the first group of schools partnering with Project GRAD in the Houston Independent School District.

CHAPTER FIVE

FINDINGS AND
LESSONS LEARNED

*There is something spiritual about this work. . . .
There is broad recognition of the seriousness
of the state of youth. . . . It is very clear to
me that there is a movement initiated by
ordinary citizens to educate in a broader sense.
There is an impatience that is urging people
on to action past fear, reluctance, waiting
for permission, or waiting for K-12 to
figure it out.*

Mary K. Boyd

The findings and lessons learned through the community educators research suggest that local communities and their citizens have a significant role to play in educating and developing young people. In fact, it is essential for a community to ensure the development of youth into contributing citizens, as the continued viability of the community depends on its next generation. The study also implies that systemic cultural change is essential for democratic communities. Fortunately, even in the early stages of our study, it was evident that significant change is underway for many communities where youth-development programs are having an impact—the kind of change that leads to a positive future for the community and for democracy.

After the first two research conversations, with two different sets of participants, we came to see that the primary focus of these community educators was youth development, not education. As mentioned in Chapter 3, participants initially did not see themselves as educators or the work that they did as educating; they saw education as the job of schools and professional educators. Once introduced to the term of *community educators*, however, they began to see and refer to themselves in that way.

Based on these interactions and later research conversations, we also learned that the community educators described tensions between schools and their programs, but they did not necessarily blame the schools for those tensions. They said their frustration with schools was that bureaucracy and red tape often made it difficult to collaborate. At the same time, however, participants acknowledged that schools were often essential to the success of their programs.

As our research conversations evolved, the inquiry deepened our discussions to include additional questions:

- What resources are available in communities to educate new generations of young people? How do community educators use the community's resources to educate young people? To what extent does the community see itself as a resource for educating youth?

- To what extent do these programs broaden the definition of education to include both the learning that occurs in school and continuous learning that occurs beyond the school building?

In our research, we did not collect enough conclusive evidence about how or whether these programs influence economic development. We did, however, discover that in many instances, positive youth development created outcomes for positive community development. The data also suggests that a citizen focus on youth development and education indicates democratic practices at work.

For example, the Albion, Michigan, Youth Development Coalition grew out of a broad community concern about the growth and development of local youth, and ultimately engaged citizens and all sectors of the community—faith-based organizations, businesses, foundations, hospitals, youth, teachers, the president and students from the local college, the local school superintendent, and others. The Albion effort was distinguished by its deliberate and intentional focus on education. The coalition hired a local citizen to coordinate a citywide effort that connected all learning experiences and engaged all sectors of the community. Among the citizens of Albion, there was a groundswell of participation in this effort, which was committed to transforming education—not just schools—in their community.

Albion is an example in which youth development ended up leading to community development. Joyce Spicer, a health-care professional; David Farley, a retired community foundation executive; and Harry Bonner, a youth advocate; seemed to agree that while some of the activities of the program initiative have shifted, the goal—building a community focused on youth—was achieved.

Citizens throughout Albion volunteered to teach classes, to provide young people with learning experiences. The health department collaborated with the high school to create programs that supported new young mothers and encouraged them to graduate and prepare for college. The intensity of the Albion program seemed to exemplify that children and youth development are everybody's business.

From what we learned about the programs involved in the community educators research, it seems clear that such community educators programs, along with the broader community, have a significant role to play in the development and education of youth. Community educators programs take a wide variety of approaches to supporting youth as they develop into competent, confident, contributing citizens. While professional educators and schools may focus on the achievement gap, these programs focus on the gaps in other essential areas, gaps that make a difference in, for example, socialization, emotional intelligence, character development, and ability to form adult-youth relationships. Further, we learned in the study that the work of community educators on these gaps can have carry-over effects that positively influence citizenship, behavior, and academic performance.

We noticed that the community educators generally did not refer to the achievement gap but seemed to understand that other matters are also important in the development of youth. Therefore, when they are involved in such community-development programs, youth are virtually ensured a greater level of readiness for academic performance and success as productive citizens. The community educators suggest that addressing issues like hunger, self-esteem, confidence, and cultural identity also enhances young people's ability to learn.

Beyond addressing these gaps, in our research we noticed other positive outcomes from youth-development programs. For instance, many young participants developed leadership skills and engaged in civic learning. Relationships in the community change in important ways, spanning old cultural and social boundaries between youths and adults.

Significantly, adults and young people in such relationships began to perceive each other differently—and more positively. Furthermore, programs that reported such adult-youth relationships also reported improved behavior and academic performance among students. Positive outcomes like these have implications not only for youth development and education, but also for a change in perceptions of youth among adults communitywide.

Another positive outcome for many youth participants is an increased sense of pride in their heritage—not just for its own sake, but as a foundation for achievement. In a research conversation, for example, Mary K. Boyd, a former school executive in St. Paul,

Minnesota, shared her work with high school girls whose parents and grandparents lived in an urban neighborhood that essentially no longer exists because of urban renewal. Rondo was a vibrant African American neighborhood in St. Paul, until the late 1950s, when it was bulldozed to make way for an interstate highway. The project displaced and dispersed residents, separating them from familiar neighborhood relationships and values.

Boyd and others who grew up in Rondo remembered how their neighborhood provided them with a sense of who they were, as individuals and as a community. They also realized that young people, their own offspring, did not have the same sense of "connectedness" to the places where they lived. In recent decades, these and other former residents have made a concentrated effort to revive the spirit of Rondo through music, arts, and other cultural events and to impart that vitality of spirit to the next generation. Their effort aims to teach the values that were the foundation of the Rondo community, and to support young citizens as they learn about and embrace their cultural identity. The experiences are providing young women with a sense of where they come from, and inspiring them with the strength and community values that supported their parents and ancestors before them.

Lessons Learned

Participants in the community educators research conversations and respondents to the survey articulated a number of lessons learned that provided a different lens through which to view education and youth development, echoing what participants had shared when I made site visits to several of their programs. Together, their observations consistently pointed to a broader definition of education and the public's role in educating youth. This shed light on the potential for an innovative, informal, organic "curriculum" that addresses the needs of the whole child, rather than focusing narrowly on academic achievement. Such a curriculum is the foundation of community educators programs that address the essential basics youth need to function effectively and to their highest potential—to become, in short, contributing citizens.

Following are some of the key lessons learned, as discussed in research conversations and mentioned in the Community Educators Survey.

Education Is Broader than Schooling

Community educators programs contradict the perception that the only resource for educating young people is schools. Community educators broaden the definition and meaning of education through their work with youth in their communities.

Citizens Educate Youth

Individual citizens, civic and social organizations, businesses, artists, activists, parents, elected officials, libraries, museums, and other institutions—all educate and make a difference in the development of youth and their communities.

Citizens Address Gaps Other than the Achievement Gap

Citizens do this because they are deeply concerned about the gaps that make it harder for youth to learn as they should and to reach their potential. Citizen educators recognize that these gaps must be closed in order to educate and develop the whole child. Some gaps are the result of history, local traditions and customs, relationships, and practices, while others may be influenced by poverty, health issues, lifestyle and home life, media, access, inequities, social pressures, and so on. Given the information gathered from the research conversations and the survey analysis, these programs may be the bridge that supports young people to access their full capacity to learn and improve both academic and social performance.

Program Leaders Are Passionate about Youth Development

Many program founders created programs to make better experiences for today's youth than they themselves had when they were younger. Features of these programs often reflected an issue or problem the founder had encountered in his or her youth.

Programs Confront Obstacles

Challenges for these programs include acquiring adequate funding, getting through the red tape and bureaucracy of schools, maintaining qualified staff, recruiting enough qualified mentors, and attracting youth participation and parental involvement.

Other notable lessons learned in the community educators study demonstrated an observable relationship between youth development and community development.

Youth Development Is Community Development

Youth-development programs foster community development, partnerships, collaborative initiatives, and relationships that span the usual boundaries of race, culture, and socioeconomic background.

Youth Are a Resource

Community education programs provide young people with opportunities to engage in social-political action and community decision making. These kinds of opportunities can be self-perpetuating, as youth are then able to contribute meaningfully to their own communities, often by helping other young people through the programs that had originally helped them.

Citizens Educate Youth After School

Community educators work with young people after school hours. It appears that programs are restoring public ownership and responsibility for educating the next generation. Citizens experience a renewed sense of their role in public education.

Using the Lessons Learned

The community educators research is not an empirical investigation; it does, however, offer a plethora of qualitative and quantitative data. The sample size is small and dedicated, to enable us to gain insight from a set of similar respondents who met the same criteria, most notably that all participants were focused on after-school youth development. The anecdotal information shared through self-report, participants' stories, experiences, and challenges are valuable examples of how programs like these work. The richness of the study comes from the face-to-face interactions of participants discussing their experiences, sharing their wisdom and insights into larger issues, such as the role of the public in public education and the relationship between democracy, education, and community.

The findings from both the online survey and the research conversations raise significant questions that other researchers and communities may wish to pursue further. Most important, the findings are an invitation for communities, citizens, community educators, school administrators, and classroom teachers to examine these outcomes in conjunction with their own visions for the education and development of youth.

In this study, the findings support community engagement, indicate the potential for civic learning in communities, and offer a means by which a community can examine itself. And, while the research does not necessarily lead to any broad generalizations or conclusions, it is encouraging with respect to what is happening in the communities studied, and what might happen in other communities. It can, that is, provoke creative reflection and discussion and serve as a resource for other communities.

Bridging Gaps

Participants in the May 2008 research conversations discussed in depth the ways they sought to meet the needs of the whole child by bridging gaps other than the often-cited academic achievement gap. As KF research associate Lara Rusch wrote in one listener's report, "It seemed like each community educator was working to fill a perceived gap in what they believe should be (part of) a holistic learning experience for young people. . . . Several of these organizations or programs are filling in gaps in learning or opportunity left by institutions (schools, the child welfare system, and so on) that the community members value as necessary for the 'whole child.'" Rusch observed, "In the process of trying to fill those gaps . . . organizations and other community members learn about their own roles and what else is needed."

This theme of "bridging gaps" was, in fact, evident in the responses to the Community Educators Survey. When asked to identify the primary focus and features of their program and who their programs target and serve, respondents revealed a variety of areas that may be considered gaps. Eighty-two percent reported "character development" as a feature of their programs; a number of respondents also mentioned development of social skills, positive relationships, and deeper understanding between adults and youth. The work of community educators seems to focus on the space between where the child is and academic achievement. It appears that this emphasis is on those areas that provide support, skill, and development, which are prerequisites for academic achievement and citizenship. In other words, community educators recognize certain elements (gaps) must be addressed to create a bridge that leads to academic achievement for every child.

These include gaps in opportunities for emotional, social, and physical development. These programs provide mentors who support students in their maturation and help them make wise choices and who teach youth to navigate the local agencies and institutions they come in contact with. They provide role models for students struggling with difficult life experiences; opportunities for spending quality time with responsible adults; access to systems of governance and practice working within those systems; and places for youth to engage in collective decision-making processes. These programs are working with young people from all backgrounds and economic levels to develop self-esteem, confidence, relationships with positive role models, career aspirations, and the ability to make wise choices.

Both the survey and the research conversations suggested that participants felt that teaching kids about cultural identity and community values was significant and important for helping to bridge gaps. They believe it is necessary to foster in youth a sense of who they are and where they come from, although different programs followed different paths to that end. One program, for example, was built on the idea of a vital local neighborhood, while another emphasized local connections as well as global traditions and the ancestral heritage of the youth involved in the program. In both cases, program leaders felt that such a community- and cultural-identity approach is important not only for youth development, but also because such an approach can build relationships across barriers that often separate individuals and groups within the larger community. Community educators in the research conversations seemed to agree that there is a positive relationship between academic achievement and youth with a strong sense of who they are.

Resources and Relationships: A Key to Change?

In the research conversations, we learned that the citizen educators engaged in these programs were passionate and expressed a long-term commitment to the development of youth. The most significant commonalities of these programs were the use of resources and the focus on relationship building. These findings offer insight into the question, are community resources and relationships, partnerships, and collaboration, important keys to change and the transformation of education?

Not surprisingly, basic human resources were the most important resources to any of these youth-development programs. Teachers, government officials, and political leaders all contributed to the programs, as did other citizens with special skills—or even "ordinary citizens" who find themselves in relationships that develop informally and organically. Dave Farley, a retired foundation executive from Albion, told of an elderly woman who welcomes young people into her home to play her piano. The youth are exposed to music, while they are also developing a relationship with an older adult, and, says Farley of the woman, "It's a treat for her because she is alone all day." He also shared the story of a convenience store clerk who, over time, got to know her regular customers, including several local youth who developed a habit of stopping by to visit her at work. Initially they were simply customers, but over time, the clerk began to talk with them, ask how they were doing in school, and talk about whatever was on their minds. As she encouraged them and motivated them to do well, they came to realize that she was genuinely interested in their progress.

Talking of these and other informal community educators, Farley points to "so many informal connections that could be made" in our communities to foster youth development. Yet many of these resources go untapped.

Available facilities were also key to the programs' success. The programs represented in the community educators research conversations had access to a variety of public and private spaces, through collaborations with churches, museums, libraries, colleges, schools, recreation centers, and other institutions. Other individuals in the community—like the woman with the piano and the convenience store clerk—were resources, even though they were not explicitly connected to any program.

Throughout our community educators research—in the research conversations and in the online surveys—relationships emerged as an important common element across all programs. Consistently, community educators described relationships and relationship building as crucial to their mission. In fact, in response to one true-false statement, more than 60 percent indicated that relationships with schools are necessary for their program to operate. This point of view was consistently validated in research conversations.

Nearly all of the programs were engaged in building relationships through partnerships and collaborative initiatives with other organizations; through citizen participation in the implementation and operation of programs; and through organizations or individuals who provided resources and services that directly benefited youths and the program itself.

Analysis of the survey data indicated that such relationships were necessary for connecting resources and people. In response to the survey question, "What are the three most important key areas that drive the mission of the program?" one respondent pointed out, "The need to connect people to resources, and resources to each other. The need to create an environment within the community that embraces and promotes youth development."

Is a Theory of Change Emerging?

In the early stages of the community educators research, we began to notice consistent, recurring principles and practices in the community educators work, all of which contributed to each program's ability to create change in the community's engagement in educating and developing young people. These recurring factors included core beliefs and values, ways of thinking about education and ways of educating, and particular actions and outcomes.

It seems that the principles and practices in these community educators programs consistently reflected components of a theory of change. Among these are a shared vision and mission, shared leadership, collaboration and partnership, ownership and responsibility for resolving problems, collaborative learning, and individual and collective choice that leads to action. Another significant element is long-term commitment to their mission and a realization that the kind of change they envision for the education and development of young people can only be achieved over time. And, of course, a real passion for serving youth is essential.

Several examples in community educators programs seemed to be connected to principles of change recognized in the literature of change theory.

Change Is Systemic

The change process must be systemic. This includes change in structures, such as policies and practices, relationships, and attitude. As I discussed in earlier chapters, one reason that so many education reforms have failed over the years is that they focused on one element of the community—schools. Yet for sustainable change, it is necessary to talk about transformation of education in both the community and its schools, and their relationships with one another. Ways of thinking and speaking, as well as belief systems, must be examined. That kind of shift in the individual and collective mindset enables a community along with professional educators to transform education and move beyond reforming schools alone. Parents and other community members, institutions ranging from corporations to museums, and countless individuals—all can share their gifts and talents with young people.

Community Recognizes Itself as a Resource

In the community educators programs, people from all different sectors of the community offered their skills and talents, creating a genuine resource for the development of young people. In St. Louis

Park, Minnesota, for example, the Children First Initiative focuses on building the 40 "assets," or character-building attributes, that kids need to become healthy, productive, and successful adults. The initiative urges everyone in the community to take ownership and responsibility for strengthening families and creating a more caring community for children and teens.

Authentic Communication

A capacity for authentic communication—the ability to deliberate and weigh issues and to consider different perspectives—is also critical to making change. Listening and speaking authentically, being able to say what really matters and to understand the impact of one's words—this kind of communication supports positive change. Once all different points of view are on the table, then a community can collaboratively make sound decisions that consider different perspectives and benefit the common good.

Collaboration and Partnerships

Reaching out, collaborating, and creating partnerships is crucial. In Albion, for example, citizens found that even among disparate individuals, their commonality of mission and their mutual commitment to youth were greater than their differences. As a result, relationships in the community shifted and people who had never worked together, who were otherwise unlikely even to come in contact with one another, were working together to make a difference in the lives of young people. Similarly, in Silver Spring, the Ambassadors Investing in Mentoring (AIM) program collaborated with the school district to apply for funds that supported the program, and it recruited and paid teachers to tutor after school. AIM also collaborated with local college students and professionals who agreed to serve as mentors for participating youth.

Collaborative Learning

In the community educators programs we found mentors, teachers, and other employees and volunteers working and learning together how best to reach and motivate and support the youth with whom they were all working. Youth and adults also learned from and with each other. The most significant principle in change theory is—"change is choice." Change occurs when citizens, professional educators and other members in the community, individually and collectively, choose to change and have the will to take action.

A Community Educator's Theory of Change

In ongoing research, we found that the factors that community educators described as initiating a foundation for systemic change in their communities are similar to change factors identified in an earlier assessment of a social change study completed by the Center for Assessment and Policy Development (CAPD) in Philadelphia, Pennsylvania. The CAPD study was based on an assessment of Healing the Heart of Diversity (HHD), a series of residential seminars initiated at the Michigan-based Fetzer Institute. HHD participants were largely social-change agents, including corporate executives, trainers, and others who lead diversity programs. The HHD seminars were expected to generate change in perspective and mind-set; encourage participants to examine different world views; build community; create relationships and understanding beyond differences; and change behavior, as well as professional and personal performance.

As part of their study, between 1996-1999, CAPD identified factors for change that seemed to be inherent within the HHD process. These factors resulted in change that began a transformative process in the personal and professional lives of HHD participants. The method of analysis for HHD, as with the community educators study, was both qualitative and quantitative.

Changes in factors, such as behavior, relationships, and community perspectives, are common elements between the two studies. The question that arises is: to what extent is there a theory or process for change prevalent in the community educators program strategies? Evidence seems to suggest that a process or theory of change may be inherent in the efforts of community educators and is common among the different programs involved in the study.

Data gathered from all sources and experiences indicates there are similarities within the operating principles and practices of efforts made by community educators and the theory of change factors and practices that CAPD found in the Healing the Heart of Diversity Study. Whether intentional or unintentional, in community educators programs, apparently there is a change mechanism operating. Additional examination is warranted to affirm this assumption.

A theory of change is a valuable tool for fostering a common understanding, as well as a vehicle to invent a new future. It serves as a guide that charts the way to successful outcomes over time. It provides an intentional structure to shift the familiar paradigm to new ways of thinking and a different mind-set. This was particularly evident in the new relationship and mind-set adults held regarding youth.

Participants in the community educators research reported that the components needed in order for change to occur currently exist in their programs. As mentioned earlier in this section, the elements reported as common to community educators are aligned with those described in the literature for making systemic change in organizations and in communities. The major elements that fuel sustainable change in community educators programs also include what matters to the community and a long-term commitment to achieving it; shared leadership; interaction among citizens, schools, and other sectors; and individual and collective decision making. Public ownership and responsibility, collaboration, partnerships and collaborative learning; and dedicated and committed action cannot be overemphasized. The community educators research offers a glimpse of what is possible. However, to transform education, making substantive and sustainable change for our youth cannot be achieved by schools alone, nor can it be accomplished by the community alone. Schools and the community must change together.

Through collaboration and partnership, these programs are building relationships and developing community, reducing barriers for youth and providing diverse experiences, creating a consciousness and awareness for others about youth, and making a positive difference in adult and youth relationships. They create strategies to work through challenges and obstacles. Finally, community educators are making things happen. These programs are having a positive impact on youth and community development and shifting perceptions and attitudes in communities about youth and changing relationships between adults and youth.

Impact from the Findings and Lessons Learned

In the community educators programs, youth are able to build relationships through which the community comes to see them as assets and resources. These transformational relationships reach across boundaries and barriers between diverse young people and adults. As a result, the programs' habits of collaboration, collaborative learning, and a focus on youth development in turn creates a positive environment for learning that benefits youth development in school and in the community. The following questions might serve as a catalyst to conversation about relationships in your community:

- In your community, what is adults' perception of young people?
- How would you describe youth and adult relationships in your community? To what extent do these relationships impact youth growth and development?
- What partnerships and collaborative activities, if any, exist in your community to support the education and development of youth?
- What resources are available in your community? What is being used?

Through youth-development programs—in the community educators study and through others like them—young people are experiencing and practicing important citizenship and leadership skills, as they develop increasingly solid relationships with adults and with each other. They are having their voices heard and authentically participating in political decision making. Cultural identity, self-esteem, and self-confidence are at the root of the community educators' intention to educate the whole child. It is clear that these programs effectively communicate that youth are everybody's business.

At the heart of positive development and learning in children is the presence of caring adults who cultivate nurturing, reliable, and safe relationships with them. As James Comer, professor of child psychiatry at the Yale University School of Medicine's Child Study Center has often asserted, "No significant learning occurs without a significant relationship."

Building such relationships is at the heart of Friends for Youth, Inc., a Redwood City, California, program that focuses on building long-term, one-to-one relationships between youth and caring adult mentors. Young people are referred to Friends for Youth by teachers, probation officers, or other youth professionals who consider them at risk of not reaching their full potential because of challenges they face at home, at school, and in their neighborhoods. Although a one-to-one relationship is the fundamental key to a mentoring program, it is also important that when young people come to Friends for Youth, they are welcomed into a kind of community that gives them a safe space to grow and explore the world. Through its Mentoring Institute, Friends for Youth also helps other agencies adopt and tailor its successful mentoring model, enabling even more youth to benefit from a consistent, caring, and safe mentoring relationship.

A STORY FROM THE FIELD

Building a Learning Community through the Power of Mentoring Relationships

Becky Cooper

The ties that young people establish with their Friends for Youth mentors have a significant, positive impact on learning and academic achievement, as well as on their personal and social well-being. The story of Allison and her mentor Justine illustrates this connection.

At the age of 13, Allison was already involved with gangs, having difficulties at home, and getting in trouble at school. Fortunately, her school counselor, who had referred many students to Friends for Youth over the years, connected Allison with the organization. Friends for Youth, in turn, matched her with a mentor named Justine—whom Allison would later describe as "like an angel sent from heaven because she came into my life when I was all alone and had no way out."

> ❝ I will never forget the day that I was opened up to the world . . . the day I met my mentor."
>
> *Karen,* a Friends for Youth mentee

As time passed and Allison grew up with Justine's support and guidance, her life began to change. Justine became both friend and family for Allison, someone she knew she could trust and count on, someone who opened up a world that Allison hadn't known before. As Allison explains, "I started going places I had never gone before. I met new people, and I got into sports. My bad grades turned into As and Bs. I graduated from high school with honors and received an award for community service. I never thought I could have done this."

As Allison looks back on her youth, she says that without her mentor, she "could have gone to jail, dropped out of school, and been involved in gangs." Instead, she has a life of opportunity and hope that illustrates the important ripple effects of a mentoring relationship. "Now I go to college," Allison says with pride, and just as important, "I am setting an example for my younger brothers and sisters."

Justine's life was also greatly enriched by her friendship with Allison. "When I signed up," she explains, "I thought I would be the one pouring into Allison's life, but I'm positive that I've gotten as much, if not more, from the relationship. Our friendship has brought a unique perspective in my life that I would never have imagined."

Like Justine, many Friends for Youth mentors come from a relatively privileged background, but with an instinct for helping others. Justine, for example, says she signed up to be a mentor after graduating from college in order to share all of the blessings she had received in life. Some mentors, on the other hand, are inspired to help because they themselves had seen in their own young lives the power of a positive relationship with a caring adult. The story of Julio and Dan exemplifies the kind of transformative power that can inspire young people to excel as they learn and develop into thriving, contributing adults.

Julio was matched with his mentor, Dan, a bank manager, nearly 30 years ago. Reflecting back, Julio says that what he remembers about his youth is "being utterly directionless." He earned nothing better than a C in school because he "just didn't care." Then his relationship with Dan helped turn him around, both personally and academically. Years later, when he graduated third in his class from the USC School of Medicine, Julio gave Dan and Friends for Youth a lot of credit, explaining that "Dan gave me his time and his friendship, but most of all he inspired me and gave me the first glimpses of what I could do with my life. He helped me develop my own dreams." Julio also describes another important lesson he learned from his mentor's example: "I always knew Dan got involved with Friends for Youth in order to give a part of himself to help his community. That is a value that lies deep within me now; it is why I chose to devote my life to medicine."

Dan himself had learned the value of giving back years earlier, when he first arrived in the United States as a teenager from El Salvador. "I needed someone to show me the ropes," he explains, "so I adopted parent-like figures whom I cast as role models." He saw in Julio the same need for a father figure to help him adjust to his new culture, and Dan was happy to play that role for him. "I'm not saying Julio wouldn't be where he was today without me, but he's better off because of what I did." Significantly, Dan says that their relationship continues to this day: "Julio will always be in my close cadre of friends."

Stories like those of Allison and Julio are not surprising, given the well-documented role of relationships in successful youth development and education. Through decades of research and experience, in fact, developmental psychologists, learning theorists, and other educators have concluded that relationships, connections, engagement, and participation are key elements in successful learning. They agree that children learn as they experience everyday life, with the help of formal and informal teachers and guides in the community. Addressing specifically the mentor-mentee relationship in their research, professor of psychology Jean Rhodes and professor of Community Health Sciences David Dubois assert that successful, effective programs rely on the establishment of close, enduring connections that promote positive youth development. Psychologist Urie Bronfenbrenner succinctly explains the key ingredient for successful youth development: "Someone's got to be crazy about the kid."

Organizations like Friends for Youth strive to apply this

amalgamation of knowledge from research and practice to establish and strengthen natural communities of caring and learning for youth. Since its inception in 1979, the organization has matched nearly 1,900 youth with caring, one-to-one mentors, and its Mentoring Institute, founded in 1998, has allowed the organization to reach many more. Through training programs, educational product development, and an annual mentoring conference, Friends for Youth has directly and indirectly served more than 2,500 agencies representing nearly two million children and youth. In those vast numbers lies one simple fact: at the very heart of a caring, learning community is one adult reaching out to mentor one child. Each of us, like Justine and Dan, possesses talents, knowledge, and resources that can make a profound impact on a child's life journey.

> *One life lesson among many I was able to come away with from my friendship with my mentor is that the best classroom we have is in our own backyard, and the best teachers are the people we meet along the way."*
>
> Chris, a Friends for Youth mentee

Becky Cooper— is an established expert in mentoring and serves as executive director of Friends for Youth, Inc., headquartered in Redwood City, California. Friends for Youth's programming has been called "the gold standard" by national mentoring researcher Dr. Jean Rhodes. Becky has trained mentoring practitioners internationally and has co-authored several publications on best practices and youth safety. Becky served on California's Governor's Mentoring Partnership Quality Assurance Standards Committee, was a guest at the White House at a Mentoring Ceremony hosted by First Lady Hillary Rodham Clinton, was inducted into the San Mateo County Women's Hall of Fame for her dedication to youth mentoring, and served on the national Mentoring Children of Prisoners Support Center Advisory Board.

The names of mentors and mentees have been changed.

CHAPTER SIX

IMPLICATIONS FOR FURTHER RESEARCH AND COMMUNITY ACTION

Some professionals in education know they need a responsible public but there isn't one in their community; they are too hard pressed by day-to-day problems to spend time on public building. I can imagine at least the broad outline of a type of collaboration that would not take professionals out of their customary routines, yet would increase the capacity of citizens to do public work in education. It involves aligning professional routines with democratic practices. Admittedly, "aligning routines" sounds vague. It could mean anything from being more communicative to actually bringing citizens into administrative meetings and classrooms.

David Mathews
Reclaiming Public Education by
Reclaiming Our Democracy

Dedicated leadership, along with a strong vision and clear mission, seemed to contribute to an organization's ability to change its citizens' thinking and perspective about youth. Leaders of such groups described new positive relationships between youth and adults and cross-cultural relationships among citizens previously separated by social, economic, and other cultural boundaries. In almost every case, relationship seemed to be the fundamental principle upon which the successful program was based. These programs not only brought together members of the community from different backgrounds but also with different perspectives and ideas. What worked and seemed different from "business-as-usual" were the relationships formed between youth and adults and diverse members of the community, where boundaries of difference were collapsed.

The successful programs set a pattern for continuous, collaborative learning that contributed noticeably to changes in how young people and adults related to one another. It seems that as both adults and youth took full responsibility for and ownership of the programs, their actions resulted in new relationships, an openness to different perspectives, a space for new leadership, and greater opportunities for youth leadership and enhanced academic performance. At the same time, these programs led to positive outcomes in community development and improved adult perceptions of youth.

Community educators programs are getting different, positive results in youth development by engaging in supportive youth and adult relationships. They are focused on acknowledging youth as an asset and a resource in their own education and development, and they are encouraging peer relationships in ways that youth learn both from and with each other. They are preparing youth as leaders, social activists, and peer mentors, and helping them to become responsible for their own learning.

Perhaps the elements discussed above might serve as a catalyst for further study on how communities achieve systemic, sustainable change. This chapter is intended to encourage an exploration of these ideas, individually and collectively. It weaves the findings, assumptions, and thinking that underlie the community educators programs that were involved in the community educators research.

Implications for Community

As you read, you are invited to examine the implications of this book in connection with the status, challenges, and successes of youth development in your community. Also, you may choose to explore the questions:

> To what extent is your community a resource to develop and educate its youth? In what ways, if any, does youth education and development in your community further democracy and democratic practices?

Relationships

In our community educators research, participants reported that citizens worked effectively together when focused on youth development. They were able to set aside racial, economic, and cultural differences to achieve a unifying result. This finding suggests that youth development and education may be a mutual concern for all citizens and is therefore less polarizing. Two questions for further study might be:

> To what extent can citizens and schools collectively commit to resolving a core community concern, youth development, and education? How can this commitment also be a source for building and sustaining diverse relationships?

Funding

"Back in the day," the informal education of youth was part of the normal fabric of life and community culture. An overt investment of community resources was not needed to create these opportunities; they naturally occurred within neighborhoods and communities. Yet when asked about obstacles and challenges, the community educators consistently responded: "funding, funding, funding." One survey respondent, speaking of funding, indicated that the challenge was "helping funders and systems understand the comprehensive nature of our work and what children and families need."

Most programs were committed to long-term existence. Many found it was necessary to request program operational funds each year. Some community educators programs received institutional funds, most often from the local government. Other programs received state and federal funds, while others received foundation grants, donations, or corporate sponsorship. Some programs had multiple revenue streams.

The concern about funding sources begs the question, does the community see itself as a resource? We learned in the research conversations that in educating youth, the community often does not see itself as a resource. In the survey, however, community educators identified a number of resources that the community provides, from mentors to program facilities.

Are the larger questions, then:

> How can these programs be certain they have adequate resources for program operation and implementation, and what role might the community play in this? To what extent is the community the source for both fiscal and human resources? If the education and development of youth became the focus of the whole community, to what extent would that make a difference, if any, in these programs having adequate fiscal and human resources?

The Community as a Resource

One of the most significant implications of this study is that, while the data strongly indicate that the community is an important resource for educating young people, the community often does not see itself as such. Citizens—including youth-program directors, staff, and volunteers—do not view themselves as educators or see their work as educating young people. In fact, the community was a primary resource for these programs in a number of ways, as, for example, when programs collaborated with individuals or with institutions like museums, municipal governing agencies, schools, and businesses.

Broadening the Definition of Education

The narrow prevailing view—that education equals schooling—leaves the professionals backed into a corner, having to concern themselves only with standardized, high-stakes exams. These programs suggest that the community, in partnership with schools, can broaden the scope of education by addressing those other gaps that must be closed in order for young people to succeed academically.

> To what extent are community educators the significant people who provide a nurturing network of support to the youth in their community? What is required for youth development to work in your community?

In the community educators study, we found community educators tutoring, mentoring, delivering nutritious food, providing character and social-skills development, and providing human resources to close the gaps beyond the achievement gap.

The pressure for students to pass high-stakes tests generates a fear in communities that learning in schools is limited to what is on the tests. Yet in fact, both school and community are concerned with the education and development of the whole child. Therefore, a significant implication of this study is that school and community partnerships are a viable and essential strategy for such youth development and education. The question is, then:

> How can communities and schools act together to address the needs of the whole child, close the gaps, and increase academic achievement? Could schools and communities acting together in this manner broaden the definition of education, and facilitate the communities' ability to hear the voices of diverse perspectives?

A Culture of Learning

Does "engaging the public" imply that communities can establish a culture of learning? David Mathews, raised a thought-provoking question about these community educators programs: "Are these programs a prelude for a culture of learning in these communities, and if so, what is a culture of learning in a community, and what does it take for citizens to create a culture of learning that fosters a 'working democracy'?"

Most of the current research on creating a learning culture is found in organizational-development theory. However, if this has value for bringing the whole community together to focus on youth development, this literature may be useful. In "The Seventh Rule: Creating a Learning Culture," for example, author and leadership expert Michael Maccoby describes what it takes to create such a culture in organizations. Individuals in such an organization, he writes, "take responsibility and support one another. They share experience and learn from mistakes as well as successes. Good ideas are heard, acted on and rewarded." These observations lead us to two questions: can Maccoby's thinking about optimizing a culture of learning be applied to communities? and who should be involved in that conversation?

In a learning culture, communication and relationships are very important. Creating a learning culture in a community means a shift in ways of believing, thinking, and doing at all levels and in all sectors. If this is so, then a shift in the thinking and practices in a community would mean that the education and development of youth would be a central focus of every citizen in every dimension of the community—not just of schools.

In "Linking At-Risk Students and Schools to Integrated Services," researcher and author Atelia Melaville writes, "Although young people spend much of their time in school, a variety of other community institutions share responsibility for creating the conditions in which young people can succeed." It appears that when schools and community collectively take responsibility and ownership of youth development and education, they establish the essential conditions for a culture of learning. Melaville also points out the key role school superintendents have in developing collaborative initiatives and partnerships. She quotes Alonzo Crim, former superintendent of public schools in Atlanta, Georgia, and the first African American to serve as school superintendent in an urban, Southern school district. According to Crim, "Superintendents need to aggregate power to get things done for children. We need to put things together, coordinate, collaborate, and provide a vision and a forum to talk about these issues."

When he came to Atlanta in 1973, Crim began to create a broad-based coalition of stakeholders whose mission was quality education for every child, regardless of race or background. At the time,

Atlanta Public Schools had just initiated its plan for racial desegregation, the Atlanta Compromise. In the midst of this social change, the superintendent stepped up to the plate to create a community that believed in and cared about every child in the school district. This Atlanta coalition, Crim's "Community of Believers," consisted of diverse groups of individuals, organizations, business leaders, and corporations. These stakeholders invested time, energy, and money in the potential of the youth in their community and, in the process, substantially broadened the meaning and understanding of education. By 1986, student performance levels in basic skills were higher than the national average. School attendance and graduation rates had risen measurably.

In addition to Crim's overall accomplishments, I am struck by the way he went about achieving them: he created a communitywide focus and collaboration on education and youth in a large, urban school district. He believed that "every person in the total community is a stakeholder and has a vested interest in the Atlanta Public School System." Crim's legacy to education is the idea of a culture of learning that depends on a community of believers who are committed to sharing ownership and responsibility for quality education for every child. He himself exemplified that commitment: in stark contrast to the usually brief tenure of big-city school superintendents, Alonzo Crim stayed in Atlanta for 15 years, passionately committed to the success of the district's children.

The elements described by Michael Maccoby as required to establish a culture of learning, as well as the belief of Alonzo Crim, that all children can learn, are noticeably present in the community educators programs described in this book. Given the results produced in Crim's Atlanta—a culture of learning and the results of community educators programs with similar elements, there is evidence that a culture of learning creates the conditions for student achievement.

- In what ways do programs like the community educators programs for youth development contribute to a culture of learning?

- In your community, what collaborative initiatives already exist? How can they be a foundation for establishing a culture of learning?
- How does this affect the way democracy works in your community?
- What does this suggest about the importance of the relationship between community and school?

School-Community Relationships

One implication of the community educators study may be that the key to creating a thriving school-community partnership is to successfully join the many separate parts into a connected whole. Such a partnership requires the coordination and cooperation of professional educators and schools; faith-based organizations, museums, and libraries; civic, social, and service organizations; police and fire departments; local governments and businesses; and private citizens throughout the community.

Unfortunately, in the past 30 years or more, a breach that separates schools from their communities seems to have widened. So the questions become, to what extent can the community and school reconnect to share responsibility—

with each fulfilling their particular roles—for educating young people? To what extent can they overcome obstacles, such as school bureaucracies and red tape or reluctant, inaccessible administrators?

While community educators naturally think beyond schools to potential resources in the community, they do not dismiss the importance of schools and professional educators. In the Community Educators Survey, respondents said that in their programs, teachers and community mentors were the primary resources for educating youth. In fact, 91 percent of the respondents selected mentors as the primary resources used to educate, while 75 percent selected teachers. (Of the 13 possible responses to this question, participants were asked to check all that apply; therefore respondents could check more than one answer. See the chart on p. 157.) Participants in research conversations also noted over and over that schools were important resources for their programs.

On the other hand, when the survey asked about challenges to program implementation, six primary obstacles emerged, with schools receiving the third most-frequent mentions (tied with "too

Community Resources Used

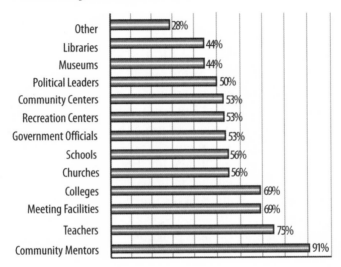

few mentors"). Individual survey comments indicated that relationship building with schools was a challenge and that there was a need for systemic change. It was mentioned that school personnel often have competing agendas and that the school testing schedules were restrictive. One survey respondent mentioned that leadership turnover within public education systems was an obstacle, as it interfered with program leaders' ability to build long-term relationships with school personnel.

The ambiguity of some of these findings invites further examination. For instance, beyond any past experiences mentioned, including red tape and bureaucratic practices, the data suggest that schools are important to community educators. The questions are:

How can they work together productively to educate and develop the next generation of contributing and competent citizens? To what extent can the combined efforts of school and community address all of the gaps—not just the achievement gap—that hinder academic performance? And taking the question a step further, how might this arrangement work to advance the practice of democracy?

Implications for Democracy

The community educators programs engaged the public in an intentional and meaningful way in educating and developing youth. Yet what we found were few programs focusing on youth development where everybody in the community was involved. Rather, most of the programs were independent, stand-alone organizations, with a few exceptions. According to the "Community Educators Initiative Survey Analysis," "Nearly all programs were involved in collaboration with some other entity (94 percent)." Participants' collaborations, according to the survey, "include education (local schools, universities, and boards of education), faith-based organizations, health providers, city government agencies, local businesses, and youth-serving agencies." Nevertheless, in most cases the collaboration was limited, and the successes these programs reported tended to cluster around the specific mission of the program. In few communities was the issue of youth development an overarching, communitywide concern—in contrast to Alonzo Crim's Atlanta, where a "Community of Believers" demonstrated democracy at work in a community that came together with a single-minded commitment.

Of the few community educators programs that had a communitywide focus, three were initiated by a mayor or city manager. Another was inspired by a college president, along with business and community leaders. One was initiated by an individual citizen. The approaches varied, from a general call for a gathering of community members, to city officials convening a number of stakeholders from different organizations and sectors of the community to create a plan for helping local youth.

In community educators programs, the role and level at which citizens are engaged gives rise to further consideration of what is a meaningful role for the public in education. This question of roles has implications for democracy in practice, locally, from community to community. The community educators programs we encountered in our research varied widely in the details of their structure and function. Nevertheless, the operations of community educators programs indicate similar ways in which they may impact democratic practices.

Most of the programs supported the efforts of young people to have a voice in the community and its decision-making processes, particularly regarding issues that impact their lives. Such efforts can have a significant impact by creating habits of self-governance and democratic participation. The stories of the Teen Center in Hampton, Virginia (pp. 66-68, and of the Mestizo Arts and Activism Center in Salt Lake City (pp. 98-104) provide vivid illustrations of the ways in which programs can help young people, who then go on to help others.

For the most part we found programs that had been started and operated by passionate individuals or nonprofit independent organizations. Although they used different approaches to planning and implementation, most of the founders started their programs in response to a broad concern about youth issues and youth development. While these programs engaged other citizens, volunteers, organizations, and institutions in the community, it is not clear that they used deliberation to define a communitywide youth agenda. In the end, although they may have grown out of a communitywide concern, the response seldom involved true communitywide efforts.

In one Kettering research conversation, for example, participants from one Virginia city told of a number of stakeholders who met several times to discuss "the problem." It seems their discussions were intended as a preventive measure: community members had noticed an increase in youth vandalism and other crime in contiguous cities, and a few such incidents in their own city. Anticipating the possibility of more serious problems at home, the community came together to identify what they needed to do to create opportunities for positive youth development. This initial effort gave birth to a number of programs started by individuals and municipal organizations, all of which operated independently, without necessarily connecting with each other. It seems that while the community had a common concern, in practice, people worked independently to address it.

Several questions naturally emerged from our work with community educators programs. For example:

How does the community create or engender the opportunity and experience for individual and collective thinking about education? And second, how do the programs include opportunities for youth to engage in activities like voting, working with elected officials to plan strategies for youth voices to be heard, and becoming involved in decision making regarding matters that concern them? Are these activities a part of community educators programs, and if so, in what ways and to what extent? What impact do the outcomes and success levels of the programs have? And what implications does the role of such activities have for the next generation of citizens?

In our research we found that youth-development programs often ended up fostering community development that benefited more than just young people. In fact "community development" is one of the three primary program features that participants reported in the Community Educators Survey. So another question that arises is:

To what extent does communitywide focus on youth and engagement with local programs and other efforts stimulate community development and political action?

One question in the Community Educators Survey asked, "Does any of your work involve democratic practices and/or political action? If so, give your most significant example." Most of the participants responded that their programs were not engaged in political action per se. A few, however, said they were and provided examples that illustrated different ideas of "democratic practices."

Some of them described democratic practices in terms of youth engagement and service to the community and the value of collective leadership and youth leadership. One participant described lobbying state legislators as political action. Another talked about teaching political activism in the community. This program convenes an annual statewide citizenship summit where youth learn about civic action and responsibility.

Interestingly, some survey respondents said that democratic practices were not a part of their programs, yet they described activities that one would almost certainly associate with such practices and that contribute to civic learning. For example, one respondent described a trip to the state capitol, for which a caravan of buses and vans took high school students to observe the General Assembly in session. Students on the trip also met legislators, state government executives, and other state officials—including the governor and their own local district representative. Yet the same survey respondent stated that democratic practices were not a part of their nonprofit civic organization's program.

Another respondent wrote about a university-sponsored research program in an urban-suburban setting, which specifically focuses on democratic practices and political action, as a part of its community development and outreach activities. "The focus of our research and activism," the respondent wrote, "is collectively determined and directed by the concerns of young people." Youth in this program, "are involved in community political issues that include addressing institutional racism, mapping projects for documenting assets in their disinvested community." Young people in this program have themselves undertaken research to explore media representations of youth of color.

Still another respondent noted that in her community, youth are active participants with public officials, leading to greater interest in the idea of shared leadership. Through a program in a different community, young people developed a "bill of rights for youth" that was adopted in their county.

A few survey respondents reported examples of youth involvement in political action and activism, as well as examples of youth having a voice in local decision making. Still others provided examples of youth engaged in activities that increased their awareness of the democratic process at work.

Implications for Further Study and Community Action

Given the lessons learned from these youth-development programs and the reports from citizen educators, it seems possible that citizen engagement with youth development may cultivate a high quality of democratic life in a community.

> How can communities use this book to examine and discuss their role in the education and development of youth? To what extent does your community view education "comprehensively, relationally, and publicly"?

Key Finding: Common Ground for Educating and Developing Youth

As we analyzed the community educators research data, we identified common elements among the programs. Among those elements, community educators consistently reported that their programs are based on developing and educating the whole child. With that finding, we unexpectedly discovered a major point of agreement among professional educators, parents, and other citizens and those concerned with and working for the development of young people: the importance of teaching the whole child.

In Edmund Gordon's article, "Affirmative Student Development: Closing the Achievement Gap by Developing Human Capital," he raises the key question regarding implications for broadening the definition of education. Gordon asks, "What will it take to eliminate the continued educational underdevelopment of so many segments of our society—to close the academic achievement gap?" Gordon further states that our nation's children must "have access to basic human resource development capitals that support development of academic abilities: good health, intellectually stimulating life experiences, and a network of significant people who have the knowledge and experience to nurture, guide, and support them in their academic pursuits."

Gordon's words, and the conclusions of other professional educators and researchers, echo the community educators study participants' repeated emphasis on closing the gaps that go well beyond the achievement gap. Clearly, closing those gaps is the most direct and effective way to teach the whole child.

Therefore, the community educators study raises several significant questions:

- To what degree is there agreement and common ground among the different sectors of the community and professional educators, on the idea that educating and developing the whole child is of primary importance?
- To what extent are all aspects of the community committed to this concept?
- How can the emphasis on development and education of the whole child be a catalyst for reuniting the school and its community, for the public to reclaim its role and responsibility for education, and for youth to grow up in a culture of learning?

As you consider the questions above, and those that appear throughout this book (see complete list on, pp. 165-172), keep in mind that they are intended as a catalyst, to initiate open and purposeful dialogue in your community about the public's role in and responsibility for educating our next generation of citizens. Perhaps the community educators research will inspire you and others to examine the ways citizens educate and develop youth, community by community, and will encourage you and your fellow citizens, in the words of Lawrence Cremin "to think (about education) comprehensively, relationally and publically."

This book offers readers an opportunity for deeper reflection, inquiry, and action. The study itself raises more questions than it provides answers, but we invite you to consider what is offered here as an invitation to launch, among citizens in your own community, conversations about educating youth.

These conversations might include teachers and other professional educators, seniors, business people, law enforcement officials, health-care professionals, and other citizens from all sectors—as well as young people themselves. Although the participants and programs described in this book are making important changes for youth development and education in their communities, none of these ideas are presented here as models to be replicated. There are no "best practices" for you to feel compelled to use or apply in your community. Rather, the intention is to for you to consider thinking and talking in new ways about education and youth in your community.

This book clearly observes that school reform is not enough to achieve the result that everyone seems to want from education. If the goal is to prepare the next generation of citizens and leaders through educating and developing the whole child, is it not essential to move from just reforming schools to truly transforming education? *What questions need to be asked and deliberated? What is being done already and by whom? Are there opportunities for collaboration? What actions must be considered and with whom must you collaborate to transform education in your community? What other issues must be considered?*

This book in no way intends to be the answer; you are invited to engage with it, make observations, and reflect on youth in your community. Think about and embrace these ideas while you generate your own. Frame your actions in a context that is based on the reality of your unique community and your distinctive educating experiences. Together, citizens who deliberate about their particular issues, values, and ideas will discover what works best to develop and educate youth and build their community.

QUESTIONS FOR
COMMUNITY ENGAGEMENT

Community Educators: A Resource for Educating and Developing Our Youth invites and encourages you to reflect and to interact with other citizens in your neighborhoods, schools, businesses, government agencies, and other spheres where residents and educators want to ensure the successful development and education of youth in their community. This is a clarion call for action strengthened by candid conversation and considered deliberation, which results in a proud future for the next generation of citizen leaders and viable communities nationwide. Throughout the chapters in this book, I offer questions for citizens and communities to consider. For your convenience, these questions are listed together here. I invite you to consider them, along with others that you may generate in conversations in your own community, as you continue—or begin—your work to educate and develop youth.

The overarching question of this study and the Kettering Foundation's work is, what does it take to make democracy work as it should?

CHAPTER ONE

Education and Democracy

In your community:

- Who are the community educators? What do they do? What motivates them?

- What is the public's role in and responsibility for education in a democracy?

- Is there a person who had a special meaning for you in your youth, and whom you have not forgotten to this day? If so, take a moment now and remember that person. Who was it? What kind of experiences did you share? How did those experiences make you feel? What influence, if any, has this person or the experiences you shared had since that time?

CHAPTER TWO

By the 1990s, when all efforts failed to produce acceptable test scores, some large city governments were beginning to take over entire school districts. Such moves, clearly at odds with deeply held beliefs about local control, aggravated the divide between local citizens and their schools:

- What are the implications for democracy when local voices are silenced in decision making for public education?
- In public education, are schools and their communities inseparable?

As you weigh alternative solutions that seem best suited for your community, you may find it helpful to keep in mind the four underlying questions behind this study:

- How is your community a resource for the growth, development, and education of the next generation?

- What makes democracy work in your community?

- What is the relationship between democracy, education, and the public in your community?

- What is the relationship between school and community; and what examples or stories, in your community, reflect how that relationship impacts youth education and development and community development?

CHAPTER THREE

I invite you to reflect on opportunities for youth development in your own community, as well as on what role and talents you bring—or might bring—to efforts at providing such opportunities. Consider individuals and organizations you know with whom you may choose to share this work and discuss how, or whether, it may be relevant for your community. To examine the conditions and directions for your community, you and others might consider initiating an assessment of the social and cultural practices, habits, and patterns that impact youth:

- How do youth development and education help strengthen, more broadly, community development and democracy? Or do they? How does "the public" in your community take ownership and, ultimately, responsibility for the long-term development of your youth?

- Are there insights for your consideration to broaden the scope of who educates in your community?

- What are the collective cultural and social customs and traditions in your community that influence your perception of and actions with youth?

- What are your individual beliefs and attitudes about youth in your community?

- Other than school, what programs or specific actions in your community currently contribute to educating and developing young people? What specifically do they do?

- How do institutional and legal practices, policies, and requirements impact youth, and citizen engagement in their education and development? How are they beneficial? Or not?

- What do we want for the next generation of young people?

- Who would you talk to about this, and how would you engage others in the conversation? Who should be at the table?

CHAPTER FOUR

During the research conversations we examined these issues through the lens of a series of questions. Consider the following for your community:

- With what challenges do communities struggle?

- What obstacles do they face as they attempt to meet those challenges?

- How do they overcome these obstacles to move forward their youth-development efforts?

- How would you describe and explain the relationship between various sectors in your community and the schools?

- What supports or is a barrier to trust, credibility, transparency, and communication?

- To what extent are schools, parents, and citizens connected or isolated?

- Are community members unable to imagine the human and other resources they already possess that could help to meet the needs of their young people?

- Can you cite examples from your own experience that indicate that members of your community do (or do not) see themselves or their community as a valuable resource for educating and developing youth?

Questions to consider as you think about the challenges facing your community:

- How can schools and communities be supported and encouraged to find common ground with one another?

- In relationship to education, with what is your community struggling?

- With what obstacles is your community challenged? How does your community resolve these challenges and obstacles to move education forward?

CHAPTER FIVE

Based on these interactions and later research conversations, we also learned that the community educators described tensions between schools and their programs, but they did not necessarily blame the schools for those tensions. They said their frustration with schools was that bureaucracy and red tape often made it difficult to collaborate. At the same time, however, participants acknowledged that schools were essential to the success of their programs.

As our research conversations evolved, the inquiry deepened our discussions to include additional questions. Ask the following regarding your community:

- What resources are available to educate new generations of young people? How do community educators use the community's resources to educate young people?

- To what extent does the community see itself as a resource for educating youth?

- To what extent do these programs broaden the definition of education to include both the learning that occurs in school and the continuous learning that occurs beyond the school building?

- Are community resources and relationships, partnerships, and collaboration, important keys to change and transformation of education?

The following questions might serve as a catalyst to discuss relationships in your community:

- In your community, what is adults' perception of young people?

- How would you describe youth and adult relationships in your community? To what extent do these relationships impact youth growth and development?

- What partnerships and collaborative activities, if any, exist in your community to support the education and development of youth?

- What resources are available in your community? What is being used?

CHAPTER SIX

Examine the implications of this book in connection with the status, challenges, and successes of youth development in your own community. In the community educators research, participants reported that citizens worked effectively together when focused on youth development. They were able to set aside racial, economic, and cultural differences to achieve a unifying result. This finding suggests that youth development and education may be a mutual concern for all citizens and is therefore less polarizing. We learned in the research conversations that, in educating youth, the community often does not see itself as a resource. However, community educators identified a number of resources that the community provides, from mentors to program facilities:

- To what extent is your community a resource to develop and "educate" its youth?

- In what ways, if any, does youth education and development in your community further democracy and democratic practices?

- To what extent can citizens and schools collectively commit to resolving a core community concern, youth development and education? How can this commitment also be a source for building and sustaining diverse relationships?

- How can communities and schools act together to address the needs of the whole child, close the gaps, and increase academic achievement? Could schools and communities acting together broaden the definition of education and facilitate the communities' ability to hear the voices of diverse perspectives?

In "The Seventh Rule: Creating a Learning Culture," author and leadership expert Michael Maccoby describes what it takes to create such a culture. He writes, "Take responsibility and support one another. . . . Share experience and learn from mistakes as well as successes. Good ideas are heard, acted on, and rewarded."

- Can Maccoby's thinking about optimizing a culture of learning be applied to your community? Who should be involved in that conversation?

CHAPTER SIX cont.

- In what ways do programs like the community educators programs for youth development contribute to a culture of learning?

- In your community, what collaborative initiatives already exist? How can they be a foundation for establishing a culture of learning?

- How does this affect the way democracy works in your community?

- What does this suggest about the importance of the relationship between community and school?

- To what extent can the community and school reconnect to share responsibility—with each fulfilling their particular roles—for educating young people?

- To what extent can they overcome obstacles, such as school bureaucracy and red tape or reluctant, inaccessible administrators?

- How does the community create or engender the opportunity and experience for individual and collective thinking about education?

- How do the programs include opportunities for youth to engage in democratic practices, such as voting, working with elected officials to plan strategies for youth voices to be heard, and becoming involved in decision making regarding matters that concern them?

- To what extent does communitywide focus on youth and engagement with local programs and other efforts stimulate community development through democratic practices and political action?

- How can your community use this book to examine and discuss roles and responsibility and take action?

- How can the public reclaim ownership of education in your community, engaging the "whole community" to focus on the "whole child"?

COMMUNITY EDUCATORS SURVEY ANALYSIS

Patricia Moore Harbour, EdD
Harbour Center for Quality Education, LLC

Data analysis prepared by
Sharon L. Newbill, PhD
Folkstone: Evaluation Anthropology

Background

The Kettering Foundation's work focuses on the question, "what does it take for democracy to work as it should?" One part of the answer is education, which is central to our democracy. Other questions arise when one considers the relationship between education and democracy: Is public ownership of education essential to democratic life in communities? Is education broader than schools alone?

This document presents findings and insights from the data analysis of a survey of "community educators." Youth-development program directors and other citizen educators across the United States responded. The survey was administered in the fall of 2009, following a series of research conversations that began in 2007 at the Kettering Foundation in Dayton, Ohio, as part of the Community Educators Research Initiative.

The present survey study focused on a series of questions that included, Who are the community educators? What do they do? What motivates them? Who started these programs, and why?

Further, the research examined struggles and obstacles that local programs encountered. It also was important to the study for us to learn what the community's resources are for "educating" youth. Does the community recognize that it has the resources to make a difference in the lives of young people?

Other questions explored include, How do communities name the problem(s) with which they are struggling? How do they manage and deal with the conflicts that arise, and how are problems resolved in order to move forward? Finally, in relationship to the larger Kettering Foundation initiatives, we looked for examples of democratic practices and political action.

The findings from this survey are consistent with the informal research conversations that occurred prior to it. The results of the survey are detailed later in this report, but a few general insights are offered here. We learned that what we call "community educator" programs

- Operate mainly after school;
- Are initiated by individual citizens, as well as a variety of entities, including nonprofit organizations, municipalities, and alternative programs;
- Are more frequently implemented by individuals and nonprofit organizations; few were found that existed on a communitywide basis.
- Use a wide variety of community resources focused on the whole child and character development;

- Are aware that relationships matter;
- Offer opportunities that include mentoring, tutoring, and programs in the arts and cultural identity;
- Are organic, emergent, and structured, and are usually an outgrowth of some community decision;
- Begin as a strategy for addressing a community issue.

Survey and Methods of Analysis

In the fall of 2009, Patricia Moore Harbour developed and administered an online survey. Respondents were participants in the Kettering Foundation's Community Educators Research Initiative research conversations, as well as other citizen educators who had not participated in any of those sessions.

The questionnaire contained both closed-ended questions (e.g., "select all that apply" checklists, True/False statements, and "select only one" response options) and open-ended questions, which offered the opportunity for elaboration. An independent research consultant, Sharon L. Newbill, working with Harbour, analyzed the survey responses to produce the findings presented below.

Seventy four percent of those who were invited (34 of 46 persons) responded to the online survey. The results of the closed-ended questions are reported as frequencies (percentages) and depicted in charts. Only persons responding to a given question are included in the percentages (i.e., 'no response' was excluded from the analysis), which accounts for the differences in the respondent totals associated with each chart.

Qualitative data are drawn from responses to the open-ended questions, and these are italicized and de-identified in order to maintain respondents' confidentiality. The open-ended questions were exported into the qualitative software package NVivo8 (QSR International) for content analysis. Content analysis consists of a systematic data reduction procedure of coding text that entails the initial breakdown of raw text into conceptual categories. These categories are discrete and identify a particular phenomenon (e.g., community development, youth development, education, leadership, mentoring). Categories may be grouped to form a higher-order, more inclusive concept, called a theme. Themes emerge by systematically linking categories that share common meanings. Common themes may be found across questions, which can inform our interpretation of the data and deepen our understanding of the issues addressed in the questionnaire.

Organization of the Report

The report is organized into three sections. The first details the **Findings**, from the quantitative and qualitative analysis. The results are presented in a report card format, with charts displaying the data and a corresponding text reporting the highlights of the data. A Discussion section provides a comprehensive interpretation of the findings in order to provide an overview of the results that leads to the final section, **Implications for Further Study**.

Findings

The quantitative and qualitative results are present in charts, tables, and text below. The headings correspond to questions asked on the questionnaire.

Response Rate and Responder Role

Almost three-fourths of contacted stakeholders completed the online questionnaire (74%, 34 of 46). The majority of responders reported their role in the program as Director (39%).

Program Origination

Community initiative was the reason given most frequently for starting the programs (38%). Personal idea and founder's vision combined accounted for another 36%. The majority of programs held 501(c)3 status (65%), (not in chart), with the predominant funding sources being grants (88%), private donors (72%), and community sponsors (63%).

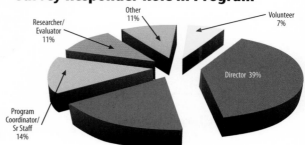

Survey Responder Role in Program

Other 11%
Volunteer 7%
Researcher/ Evaluator 11%
Director 39%
Program Coordinator/ Sr Staff 14%

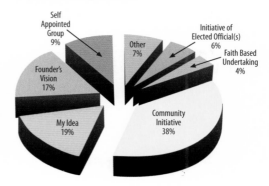

Program Origination

Self Appointed Group 9%
Other 7%
Initiative of Elected Official(s) 6%
Faith Based Undertaking 4%
Founder's Vision 17%
Community Initiative 38%
My Idea 19%

Program Site

The predominant location for the programs was in a community center (39%). Almost one-fourth of programs were held in schools, either during or after school hours (26%). The option "other" included a variety of sites, such as a fire station, health care center, and corporate facilities.

Program Site

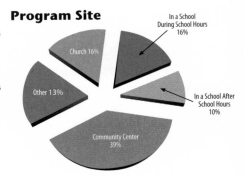

Program Focus

Mentoring, developing the whole child, tutoring, and creating a sense of community combined to account for 61% of the respondent program foci.

Program Focus

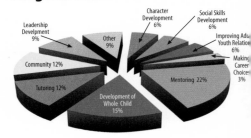

Program Target Group

Two-thirds of the programs were targeted to students through high school (and age 18 years), regardless of gender. The majority focused on youths living at or below the poverty level (59%) and academically low achieving (53%).

Target Youth

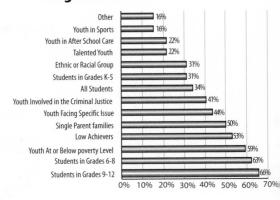

Youth Served

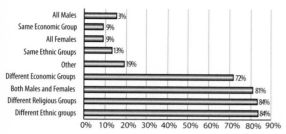

Youth Served

A checklist of demographic characteristics may offer a more representative look at the youth participating in the programs. These youth are more diverse than the target population, to include both males and females, from multi-ethnic backgrounds, and different economic and religious sectors.

Relationship with Youth

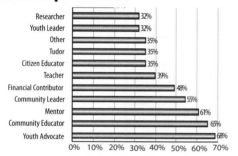

Relationship with Youth

Most respondents described their relationship with youth as advocate (68%), community educator (65%), mentor (61%), or community leader (55%).

Program Features

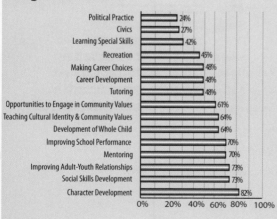

Program Features

A variety of features were offered for respondents to "check all that apply" in the questionnaire. From that list, character development was checked most often (82%). Almost three-fourths of programs featured social skills development and opportunities to improve adult-youth relationships and understanding. Civics (community government) and politics were the least emphasized in the respondent group.

Additional information on programs was captured in a series of True/False questions (see table below). The majority of respondents "believed that youth in their program learned community values that affirm their cultural and/or community identity (87%). The majority also felt that youth in their programs contributed to community development (94%), were trained for civic and/or political involvement (81%), and participated in some form of decision making for the community (74%). Through these and other activities, all respondents believed that relationship was essential to the success of their programs (100%) and that they had a positive economic impact on their communities (94%). Nearly all programs were involved in community collaboration (94%). These collaborations were varied and extensive, to include education (local schools, universities and boards of education), faith-based organizations, health providers, city government agencies, local businesses, and youth-serving agencies.

Community Resources

In another "check all that apply" checklist, community mentors (91%) and teachers (75%) were marked as the primary resources a program used to educate youth. Most programs also were heavily reliant upon local educational institutions (e.g., churches, colleges, and schools) as meeting facilities. In a True/False question about the importance of relationships with schools, 62% agreed that relationships with schools were necessary for their program to operate. Most (58%) also indicated that it was not difficult to engage school officials in their efforts, even though the school bureaucracy makes the collaboration challenging (74%).

Community Resources Used

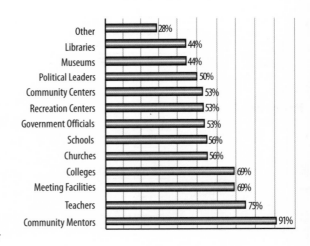

Resource	Percentage
Other	28%
Libraries	44%
Museums	44%
Political Leaders	50%
Community Centers	53%
Recreation Centers	53%
Government Officials	53%
Schools	56%
Churches	56%
Colleges	69%
Meeting Facilities	69%
Teachers	75%
Community Mentors	91%

Community-Based Features of Programs	Percent Yes
Youth participate in some form of decision making for the community.	74%
We train youth to participate in community, civic, and/or community identity.	81%
Our youth learn community values that affirm their their cultural and/or community identity.	87%
Our program has a positive economic impact in our community.	94%
Youth development has contributed to community development.	94%
We collaborate with other programs in the community.	94%
Relationships with other communities institutions and organizations are essential to the success of the program.	100%

Community Perception of Youth

Respondents most frequently characterized the community as perceiving youth to be difficult to understand (29%) or a problem (26%). Fewer (19%) placed the responsibility for youth within the community, and 13% felt youth to be an asset. In a True/False question asking about changing perceptions of youth, the majority of respondents agreed (77%) that changing adult perceptions of youth was a central focus of their efforts.

Community Perception of Youth

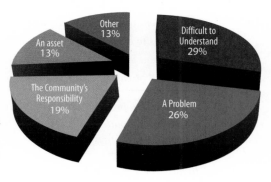

Key Areas that Drive Program Mission

Responses to this open-ended question were coded using the qualitative software package, NVivo8. As shown in the chart, the responses clustered (i.e., 7 or 8 comments each of 30 total) around Community Development, Character/Asset Building, and Academics/Education, and the associated subthemes. Therefore, four themes (with subthemes) emerged from the 30 responses to this question:

1. Community development, with the subtheme of mentoring;
2. Character or asset building, with two subthemes of cultural identity and leadership;
3. Academics and/or education; and
4. Strengthening families.

A Sampling of Respondent Comments Follows: Community development

"The need to connect people to resources, and resources to each other. The need to create an environment within the community that embraces and promotes youth development."

"The need to provide youth with positive opportunities and outlets that help them learn how to be engaged citizens."

"To have an organization that is willing to face tough challenges that arise in our community and work TOGETHER—as an organization and a community—to bring about positive change."

"Commitment to children who need a caring adult added to their current life situation to expand views of themselves and positive possibilities."

"Mentoring relationships."

Key Areas of Program Mission

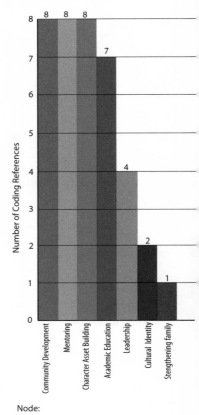

Node:

Character/asset building, with subthemes of cultural identity and leadership

> *"Cultural identity development."*

> *"Developing leadership skills."*

> *"Collective leadership to address community challenges."*

Academics/education:

> *"Our informal education program builds (1) skills, (2) knowledge and (3) attitude."*

> *"Creating a learning community; educational knowledge and access; completion of college degree."*

Problems Programs Are Working to Solve

Thirty-one persons responded to this open-ended question, which was coded into two categories: youth healthy development (8 of 31) and increasing youth capacity (6 of 31). These categories, coupled with those of "empowerment," "developmental assets," and "gang prevention," may be grouped together to form a theme of **Positive Youth Development**, which would account for 25, or 81%, of responses.

Respondent comments:

Cultural knowledge and identity, raise self esteem, critical thinking, participating in community, valuing and taking responsibility for one's own education, making good choices.

Our agency steadfastly believes in the youth-development assertions that young people who are problem free are not fully prepared, and fully prepared young people are not fully engaged. Our goal is fully prepared and fully engaged youth valued by members of the community.

Problems Programs Are Working to Solve

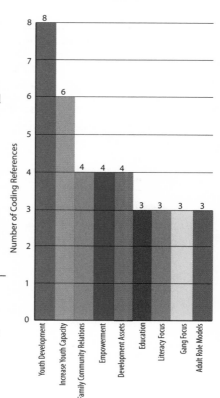

Node:

"It is an opportunity-based initiative. We are asking everyone in the community to determine ways to build on the positive things, or developmental assets, young people have."

"Self-esteem, low motivation issues along with getting students to believe that they can become successful."

"We have a big problem with our youth in gangs, they are choosing being in gangs rather than going to school."

Another (albeit lesser) theme, **Social Relationships**, was created by grouping family/community relations (4 of 31) and adult role models (3 of 31), to account for 7, or 23% of respondents. Pertinent comments include the following:

"We want the youth participating in our program to develop a positive public service mind-set, and desire to play an active, contributing role in their community."

"Relationship with students their parents, community and the direction in their lives."

"Providing caring role models for at risk youth."

A final theme, **Education**, was created by grouping the focus categories of "education" and "literacy," to account for another 6 (19%) of respondents:

"We aim to increase high school graduation, college readiness, college access, & college success for students enrolled in [Community] most economically challenged communities. We do this by working collaboratively with the school district & universities, the community, the children & their families from Pre-K through college."

"Building capacity within communities of African descent to support the healthy development of children, including children's educational, social, and cultural needs. To this end, we focus on literacy development in both children and adults as a means for building cultural identity as the foundation for successful learning and living."

Program Impact

Twenty-five persons responded to this open-ended question, which was coded as above. Three themes predominated: **Positive Youth Development** (9 of 25, 36%), **Education** (8 or 32%) and **Community Development** (5 or 20%). These themes are consistent with the problems programs are working to solve or key areas of the program mission (above).

Respondent comments:
Positive youth development

> *"We focus on ensuring that students are well-rounded and emotionally healthy."*

> *"We are developing our leaders of tomorrow and getting the community to see the value of collective leadership."*

> *"We invite everyone and anyone who wants to build assets in youth to be part of what we are doing. After being trained on the 40 assets, they in turn, train others, spread the word, identify how they already build assets and determine ways they can build assets."*

Education

> *"The students that would not have had an opportunity to be involved in learning during their exposure or expelled from the regular school system was afforded the opportunity to continue their learning and others were able to completed a G.E.D, high school diploma. Then there were students who returned to their area school at the end of their suspension."*

> *"We have demonstrated youth ability to achieve academically. For example, children in our eight-week reading instruction/tutorial program demonstrate an average of 2-5 level increase in reading levels and reading skill sets. A majority of the children enter our reading program reading below grade level."*

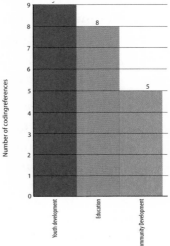

Program Impact

Node:

"We measure our impact in 4 ways: drop out reduction, high school graduation increase, college enrollment increase, college graduation increase."

Community Development

"We are a work in progress, but seek to bring the community into the realm of education with our focus on partnerships with the schools, and among agencies and organizations in the community."

"Many community members come to us for help resources and guidance."

Involvement in Democratic Practice or Political Action

Only 13 of the respondents said that their programs were involved in democratic practices and/or political action. Respondents were asked to provide an example of their involvement, and these comments were coded into actions at the 3 levels: community, state, and federal. As seen in the charts, actions involving some type of Community Development were mentioned by 7 respondents, accounting for half of all comments.

Respondent comments:

"Yes our program focuses explicitly upon democratic practices and political action. This work is both part of our own community development and also our outreach. We are actively involved in community political issues that include addressing schools' institutional racism, mapping projects for documenting assets in our disinvested community, and research exploring media representations of youth of color. The focus of our research and activism is collectively determined and directed by the concerns of young people."

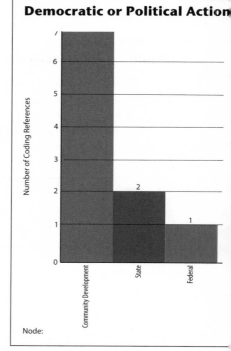

"As a community of learners we are insistent on tolerance and open-mindedness. We teach and encourage political action as a way to be involved citizens. We are a community, and as a community we believe in participation.

Every voice is heard and acknowledged, and every family in the community is a participant and contributor. We value participation over gift amount and have an annual fund which can proclaim 100% participation for each of the last five campaigns."

"Having the youth be active participants at the tables of decision makers in [A] County has opened a few eyes and a few doors to the concept and value of collective leadership. We are part of many community youth committees and support such efforts as a recent "Bill of Rights" for youth that was adopted in our county."

Obstacles or Challenges to Program Implementation

Six obstacles emerged from the responses to this question: funding, staffing, schools, mentors, youth participation (and the subtheme of parent involvement), and space. Clearly, the greatest obstacle to program implementation was funding (27 of 31, or 87%):

"Local, state and national funding, recession is keeping most investors of keeping the profits so many children with less funding being slow."

"Funding, funding, funding."

"Access to adequate funding, year to year."

"Helping funders and systems understand the comprehensive nature of our work and what children and families need."

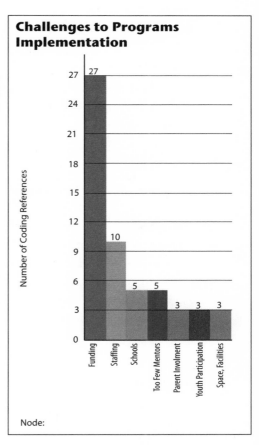

Challenges to Programs Implementation

Node:

Staffing, both number and conflicts of time for existing staff, was the second greatest obstacle (10 responses):

> *"Lack of fully prepared workforce to implement quality youth-development programs."*

> *"Staffing availability."*

> *"Volunteer time."*

Schools and too few mentors are the next most frequently mentioned challenges:

> *"Leadership turnover within public education systems."*

> *"Relationship building with schools. Need for systemic change in schools/districts."*

> *"School competing agendas."*

> *"Restrictive school testing schedules."*

"The challenge of youth (and parent) participation is captured in these comments:

> *"Lack of consistency of participants due to lack of consistency from parents."*

> *"Lack of interest by youth to participate in program."*

Discussion

Through the quantitative and qualitative analyses of this data, we are able to identify three key features of the community educator programs: Positive Youth Development, Education, and Community Development. These features are evident in many program elements, including focus, features, mission, problems working to solve, and impacts. The implication is, then, that program intentions, actions, and outcomes are congruent. The three key features can be further illumi-nated through compelling stories shared by several respondents:

Positive Youth Development

One of my former students, who is now a grown woman in college and has a child of her own, called me and told me she needed my help writing a term paper. She went on to tell that she wanted to write her paper on the African American Cemetery #2. I, being really proud of the fact that this was to be the subject of her paper, launched into a long oratory. I said, "do you remember when I took you and other Teen Center students to the cemetery and there were weeds up to your chest?" I reminded her that it was on that day we started to cut those weeds, and of our weekly outings to do the same. I asked her if she remembered how we would read the tombstones and how we had located the graves of African American jockeys who won the First Kentucky Derbies. I asked her if she knew that the cemetery was now listed as a National Historic Place, and how she was a part of making that happen. She looked at me with a blank stare and said, "Brother Bruce, why do you think I want to write about it?"

We have in our eight years had more than one student who fits the "Max" example, but he was the first and in many ways the guiding light. I accepted this student in our first year. I liked his parents and immediately liked Max. However, he was a beaten and entirely lost student. He could not look you in the eye; he could not engage in social intercourse—his head was down, his spirit broken. Though given many opportunities, he had failed academically. He had "learning differences" and focus issues. He presented to me as defeated, diffident, apathetic and miserable … but he liked to draw. Over the course of four years at Community High, Max raised his head, learned to speak in public, became a popular student and achieved academic success. He did this because he was allowed and encouraged to be an artist. Because he began to believe in his artistic ability, he was willing to work in other academic areas; he was willing to learn how to compensate for his learning differences.

This summer we held two leadership camps, one for middle school students and one for high school students. It was an incredible opportunity to be immersed in working with youth on a day-to-day basis and seeing how they can take in knowledge and information and integrate it into what they already know and believe. This experience solidified in my mind why we need to focus on youth and do more for them, and with them! The youth that were a part of these

camps enthusiastically took part in our training and the service projects they created, and asked for more. We decided to provide more
service opportunities for them based on this experience, as our community does not currently have a lead agency for youth service. We
believe that this engagement of youth will help them gain confidence
and skills that will help them beyond high school.

Education

Our work began as a business partnership with Houston's lowest
performing high school, initially offering scholarships to students.
While more students went to college, there was no evidence of systemic change. By collaborating with the community, the entire feeder
system of schools K-12, the local universities, other nonprofits, we created a model that is now achieving results. We now have over 850 college graduates. Our first high school is leading the district in positive
change of the dropout rate. Our model has been adopted in 12 other
cities, each forming its own board and responding to its community
in unique ways. Individual stories from students and families abound.
Scholars who are now teachers have returned to their community
schools to make new contributions. This past year, over 650 graduating high school seniors gathered with their families to celebrate earning our scholarship.

One of our students, who participated in our 2009 summer literacy
and cultural heritage camp, made significant connections between
reading, life, and learning—the ultimate purpose of much of our work.
This soon-to-be third-grade male student was extremely reserved at
the start of the eight-week program and had low confidence levels. By
the end of the program his confidence had grown, as did his reading skills. Weeks later he sent us a special thank you card in which he
drew pictures of his personal transformation, himself emerging out
of a book. At first he is a stick-figure in the book. Then he steps out
of the book. In a series of pictures he shows how he changes from a
stick-figure to an actual person. He told us the card was about him
stepping out of a book and becoming a "whole person." At the top of
the card, he wrote, "I Read for Life." The card showed us what happens

to the efficacy of our children when they are supported academically and culturally.

Community Development

Two years ago as high school students, Juan and Hector began a community-based action research project to examine some of the obstacles to higher education faced by undocumented students. This research determined that lack of information was a major obstacle for undocumented students' pursuit of higher education. Based on this finding, Juan and Hector have worked tirelessly over the past two years to help distribute information regarding the opportunities that do exist for undocumented students to students, families, and counselors. The main component of this work is a blog that informs undocumented students of their educational rights and to report updates on any new policies and scholarships. This is a resource to institutionalize the informal ways that students share information. Because of their own experiences navigating the education system as underrepresented students Juan & Hector know the pipeline from the inside. This is a powerful position from which to make change.

Cole and Sydney are … 4-H'ers in the Go Getters 4-H Club. Cole (age 13) and Sydney (age 11) recognized that the local hospital was throwing away socks used by patients having surgery. The socks had only been worn once and when patients didn't want them, were thrown away. Cole and Sydney worked with the hospital to save the socks. So Cole and Sydney would bring them home and wash, dry, and match them before donating them to the local homeless shelters and nursing homes. Child socks were even mailed overseas to under-privileged children. They have been doing this project for four years now.

Our Neighborhood Health Visitors (NHV) Program is creating healthy communities one neighborhood at time. NHV is a network of trained community residents dedicated to connecting Albion residents with county health resources. The goal of the program is for Albion residents and surrounding communities to have 100 percent access to health care with zero disparities. (Complete equality for everyone.) Neighborhood Health Visitors will act as community health advocates by giving a voice to the needs of residents. We found ourselves without adequate volunteers to canvass neighborhood homes, and as a result we chose a different methodology that entails hosting a Health Fair. The health fair was held in a local park with tables of information and lunch, and as you can imagine, it proved to be very successful as people came out to not only receive information but eat.

Implications for Further Study

"We want the youth participating in our program to develop a positive public service mind-set, and desire to play an active, contributing role in their community."

The Community Educators Survey offers significant insights and raises additional questions about the role and capacity of the public in education, and the difference this makes both in community development and youth development. It is clear that positive and good work is being implemented in many communities. While this study indicates community development is occurring along with youth development, it does not find significant evidence of democratic practices and political action. Although education is a key feature of the programs, there was no evidence that these efforts were targeted to what professionals call the achievement gap. Nor did we discover how conflicts are resolved in the communities.

So more can be learned, and further study may include the following:

- Identify whole communities engaged in educating and youth-development. Are schools included as part of the community? These programs in this survey reported schools are essential to youth-development programs.

- Community educators identify many "gaps" to close in order for young people to succeed, including self-esteem, leadership, food, academic assistance, positive relationship with adults, a change in perceptions of young people by the community, character development, and adult role models. How does the community create an environment that focuses on the whole child?

- How do relationships that create a public for public education engender an environment where learning is broader and inclusive of schools?

- What are the examples in such communities? How do disparate programs sponsored by individuals, different organizations, and schools in the same community come together for the purpose of learning?

- In what ways do democratic practices and socio-political action develop youth and strengthen the community? Can examples be identified?

- What is a culture of learning? What does it take for citizens to create a culture of learning that fosters a working democracy?

BIBLIOGRAPHY

Abdul-Alim, Jamaal. "Edmund Gordon, Marian Wright Edelman to Be Honored with John Hope Franklin Awards." *DIVERSE Issues in Higher Education* (2011) (accessed August 3, 2011) http://diverseeducation.com/article/14859/.

Adler, Mortimer. *The Paideia Proposal: An Educational Manifesto.* New York: Touchstone, 1998.

Annenberg Institute for School Reform at Brown University. "Educational Equity and Excellence" (accessed January 25, 2011) http://annenberginstitute.org/equity/index.html.

Bracey, Gerald. "The Market in Theory Meets the Market in Practice: The Case of Edison Schools" (Educational Policy Research Unit, College of Education, Arizona State University, 2002).

Bridgeland, John, Robert Balfanz, Laura A. Moore, and Joanna Hornig Fox. "Building a Grad Nation: Progress and Challenge in Ending the High School Dropout Epidemic." *Civic Enterprises* (2010) (accessed November 4, 2011) http://www.civicenterprises.net/ reports/ED%20-%20building%20 a%20grad%20nation.pdf.

Brown, David. "The Work of Lawrence Cremin: Who Are the 'Educators' Among Us?" Unpublished article.

Brown, Laurence D., and Jeffrey Mirel. "From Public Education to the Education of the Public." *Phi Delta Kappan* 71(8) (April 1990): 651- 653.

Cahill, Caitlin. *"Why Do They Hate Us?* Reframing Immigration through Participatory Action Research." *Area* vol. 42, iss. 2 (2010): 152–161.

Cahill, Caitlin, and Matt Bradley. "Documenting (In) Justice: Community-Based Participatory Research and Video." In *The Paradox of Urban Space: Inequity and Transformation in Marginalized Communities*, edited by Sharon E. Sutton and Susan P. Kemp. Palgrave, 2011.

Cahill, Caitlin, Matt Bradley, and David Alberto Quijada Cerecer, "Dreaming of . . . ": Reflections on Participatory Action Research as a Feminist Praxis of Critical Hope." *Affilia*. Sage Publications, 2011. http://aff.sagepub.com/content/25/4/406.

Coleman, James S. "How Do the Young Become Adults?" *Review of Educational Research* vol. 42, no. 4 (Autumn 1972): 431-439 (accessed January 23, 2011) http://www.jstor.ore/stable/1169895.

Cremin, Lawrence A. "Public Education and the Education of the Public." *Teachers College Record: The Voice of Scholarship in Education* vol. 22, no. 1 (1975): 1-12 (accessed January 25, 2011) http://www.tcrecord.org/search.asp?kw=lawrence+cremin&x= 0&y=0.

Cremin, Lawrence A. *Public Education*. New York: Basic Books, 1976.

Cremin, Lawrence A. *Traditions of American Education*. New York: Basic Books, 1977.

Cuban, Larry, and Michael D. Usdan. *Powerful Reforms with Shallow Roots: Improving America's Urban Schools*. New York: Teachers College Press, 2002.

Delaney, Bill. "Atkinson Could Take Over Scandal Ridden District." *Morning Journal*, July 7, 2011 (accessed July 14, 2011) http://www.morningjournal.com/articles/2011/07/07/ news/mj4773392.txt.

Dewey, John. *The School and Society*. Chicago: The University of Chicago Press, 1899.

Ecker, Pam. "John Dewey 1859 – 1952." Bowling Green State University Department of Education, Spring 1997 (accessed January 12, 2011) http://www.bgsu.edu/ departments/acs/1890s/dewey/dewey.html.

_____."Editorial: Schools and Community: Inseparable." Opinion. *JSOnline, Milwaukee-Wisconsin Journal Sentinel*, April 29, 2007 (accessed September 15, 2011) http://www.jsonline.com/news/opinion /29388379.html.

Edwards, Claudia L. *Who Stole Public Schools from the Public: Voices from the Mount Vernon School District*. University Press of America, Inc., 2011.

Fricke, Michael. "From the Editors: Mayoral Takeovers in Education: A Recipe for Progress or Peril?" *Harvard Educational Review* (Summer 2006) (accessed July 14, 2011) http://www.hepg.org/her/abstract/6.

_____."What's a TIF District, and Why Should I Care?" Peoria Magazines.com interBusiness Issues, July 2010 (accessed August 5, 2011) http://www.peoria magazines.com/ibi/2010/jul/whats-tif-district-and-why-should-i-care.

Gibson, Cindy. "Newark Parents Pushed Out of Decision Making on Zuckerberg Donation." *Nonprofit Quarterly* (October 10, 2011).

Glaeser, Edward L., Giacomo Ponzetto, Andrei Shleifer. "Why Does Democracy Need Education?" Harvard University and NBER working papers, October 2005.

Goldhammer, Robert. *Clinical Supervision: Special Methods for the Supervision of Teachers*. New York: Holt Rinehart and Winston, 1969.

Gordon, Edmund W. "Affirmative Student Development: Closing the Achievement Gap by Developing Human Capital." *Educational Testing Service Policy Notes* vol. 12, no. 2 (Spring 2004) (accessed December 10, 2010) http://www.eric.ed.gov/ERICWebPortal/ search/detailmini.jsp?_nfpb=true&_&ERICExtSearchSearchValue_0=ED486414&ERICExtSearch_SearchType_0=no&accno=ED486414.

Grassmann, Laura. "Mortimer Adler and the Historical Context of *The Paideia Proposal*" (October 13, 2011) http://www.library.american.edu /staff/reece/adler/adler.html.

Harbour, Patricia Moore. *Community School Bonding*. Kettering Foundation unpublished report.

Harbour, Patricia Moore. "Reclaiming Public Education" Kettering Foundation unpublished report, 2007.

Harbour, Patricia Moore. *Reflections and Observations, Reclaiming Workshop, What We Learned.* Kettering Foundation unpublished report, November 25, 2007.

Harbour, Patricia Moore. "Focus on Community, What's Changed: Are Citizens Reestablishing Education Ownership?" *Connections* (2008): 19-21.

Harbour, Patricia Moore. *What We Learned.* Community Educators Work Group Session, Kettering Foundation unpublished report, November 17-18, 2008.

Harbour, Patricia Moore. *Brief Summary of Lessons Learned: Are Citizens Re-Establishing Ownership for Educating Youth?* Kettering Foundation unpublished report, May 18, 2009.

Harding, Heather. "Supplementary Education: Educating and Developing the Whole Child An Interview with Edmund W. Gordon." Annenberg Institute for School Reform, January 2007.

Harwood Institute for Public Innovation (accessed October 26, 2011) http://www.theharwood institute.org/index.php?ht=d/Home/pid/10131.

Hess, Frederick M. "Looking for Leadership: Assessing the Case for Mayoral Control of Urban School Systems." *American Journal of Education* (May 2008).

Hill, Sara, ed. *Afterschool Matters: Creative Programs That Connect Youth Development and Student Achievement.* Thousand Oaks, CA, Corwin Press, 2008.

———. "History of the Effective Schools Movement." Lake Forest College, Donnelley and Lee Library Archives and Special Collections, Chicago's National Liberal Arts College (accessed September 7, 2011) http://library.lakeforest.edu/archives/HistoryofEffective Schools.html.

John W. Gardner Center for Youth and Their Communities (accessed September 15, 2011) http://gardnercenter.stanford.edu/.

JP Associates. "Seven Correlates Handout" (accessed August 18, 2011) http://www.jponline. com/downloads/institute/ Seven%20Correlates%20Handout%20%5BCompatibility%20 Mode.pdf.

Kettering Foundation. "Evolution of Questions about the Public and Public Education." *Continuing the Conversation, Dayton Days Research Report.* Fall 2010, 3-7.

Kinpaisby-Hill, C. "Participatory Praxis and Social Justice: Towards More Fully Social Geographies. In *A Companion to Social Geography*, edited by V. Del Casino Jr, M. Thomas, R. Panelli, and P. Cloke. Oxford: Wiley-Blackwell, 2011.

Kirst, Michael W., Katrina E. Bulkley. *Mayoral Takeovers: The Different Directions Taken in Different Cities.* Report prepared for American Educational Research Association Annual Meeting, April 2001.

Koliba, Christopher. "Democracy and Education, Schools and Communities Initiative: Conceptual Framework and Preliminary Findings." Paper for the John Dewey Project on Progressive Education, University of Vermont, College of Education and Social Services, May 13, 2003 (accessed November 9, 2010) http://www.uvm.edu/~dewey/ articles/sl sum.html.

Kretzmann, John P., and John L. McKnight. "Building Communities from the Inside Out: A Path Toward Finding and Mobilizing a Community's Assets." Asset-Based Community Development Institute, Institute of Policy Research, Northwestern University, 1993 (accessed September 4, 2011) http://www. abcdinstitute.org/docs/abcd/ GreenBookIntro.pdf.

Lezotte, Lawrence W. "Revolutionary and Evolutionary: The Effective Schools Movement" (accessed September 15, 2011) http://cascade.k12.mt.us/Pages/administration/.

Maccoby, Michael. "The Seventh Rule: Creating a Learning Culture." *Research Technology Management* vol. 42, no. 3 (May-June 2003): 59-60.

Mathews, David. *For Communities to Work*. Kettering Foundation Press, 2002.

———. *Reclaiming Public Education by Reclaiming Our Democracy*. Kettering Foundation Press, 2006.

———."Looking Back/Looking Ahead at Communities" *Connections* (2008): 4-7.

———."The Public and the Public Schools: The Coproduction of Education." *Phi Delta Kappan* (April 2008): 560-564.

McGrath, Ellie, and Ken Banta. "Education: Big Business Becomes Big Brother." *Time* November 1, 1982 (accessed February 7, 2011) http://www.time.com/time/ magazine/ article/0,9171,923062,00.html.

McKenzie, Floretta Dukes. "City Schools with Corporate Partners." *Vocational Education Journal* vol. 60 no. 8 (1985): 11-12, 40-42.

Melaville, Atelia. "Critical Issue, Linking At-Risk Students and Schools to Integrated Services." 1996 (accessed December 5, 2010) http://www.ncrel.org/sdrs/areas/ issues/students/ atrisk/at500.htm.

Mestizo Arts and Activism. "University Neighborhood Partners" (accessed October 14, 2011) http://www.partners.utah. edu/communityLeadership/mestizo.html.

Mestizo Arts and Activism. "Who We Are and What We Do" (accessed October 14, 2011) http://mestizoactivism.blogspot. com/p/who-we-are-and-what-we-do_09.html.

Mintrom, Michael. "Local Democracy in Education: The Current Situation and Future Prospects." Paper prepared for presen-tation at the 2006 Annual Meeting of the American Political Science Association, August 31 – September 3, Philadelphia, PA (accessed November 18, 2010) http://citation.allacademic. com/meta/p_mla_apa_research_citation /1/5/2/0/5/pages 152051/p152051-1.php.

Mitchell, Matt. "State and Local Economic Development Programs." Paper presented at Neighborhood Effect, Mercatus Center at George Mason University, May 3, 2011 (accessed August 24, 2011) http://neighborhoodeffects.mercatus.org/2011/05/03/

state-and-local-economic-development-programs/.

Newbill, Sharon. "Community Educators Initiative Survey Analysis." Folkstone: Evaluation Anthropology, July 2010.

Olouch, Ibrahim. "Sources of Finance for U.S. Education." *Educated Topics*. March 18, 2011 (accessed July 7, 2011) http://www. educatedtopics.com/sociology/sources-of-finance-for-us-education.html.

Olson, Katie. "Mestizo Arts and Activism Project Presents Research." *U News Center*, November 13, 2008 (accessed October 14, 2011) http://unews.utah.edu/news_releases /mestizo-arts-and-activismproject-presents-research/.

Peterson, Rodney L. Schoolhouse Museum (accessed August 2011) http://www.theschool housemuseum.com.

———. Corporations: Property Tax Abatements, Tax Increment Financing, and Funding for Schools." National Education Association Research Working Paper, 2003 (accessed August 18, 2011) http://www.nea.org/assets/docs/ HE/mf_protecting publiceducation.pdf.

———. "Power Brokers: Public Schools Takeover Proposal." *DCPS Watch*. February 18, 2004 (accessed January 9, 2011) http:// www.dcpswatch.com/dcps/040218.htm.

———. "*Reforming* or *Transforming* Education: More than Just Words." Teacher's Mind Resources 2001-2011 (accessed September 15, 2011) http://www.teachersmind.com/transform education.html.

———. "Teacher Perceptions of the Importance of Effective Schools Correlates to Improving Student Achievement." Ed.Diss. North Carolina State University, Raleigh, NC, September 15, 2011. http://repository.lib.ncsu.edu/ir/bitstream/1840.16/6674/1/ etd.pdf.

Severson, Kim. "Systematic Cheating Is Found in Atlanta's School System." *New York Times*, July 5, 2011 (accessed September 23, 2011) http://www.nytimes.com/2011/07/06/ education /06atlanta.html?ref=us.

———. "A Scandal of Cheating, and a Fall From Grace." *New York Times*, July 7, 2011 (accessed September 23, 2011) http://www. nytimes.com/2011/09/08/us/08hall.html ?pagewanted=all.

Shalash, Samieh. "Summary of John Dewey's Biography." Adapted from the *Concise Columbia Encyclopedia*. Columbia University Press, 1991 (accessed June 4, 2011) http://wilderdom.com/ experiential/JohnDeweyPhilosophyEducation.html.

———."Theory of Change: A Practical Tool for Action, Results and Learning." Organizational Research Services for Annie E. Casey Foundation, 2004 (accessed January 18, 2011) http://www.aecf.org/upload/publicationfiles/cc2977k440.pdf.

———. "Tribute to Our Legends." Georgia State University, College of Education, Alonzo A. Crim Center for Urban Educational Excellence, January 27, 2011. http://education. gsu.edu/ cuee/history.htm.

———. "Theory of Change." *ActKnowledge Theory to Results*. Center for Human Environments, March 3, 2011. http://www.act knowledge.org/theory-of-change/.

———. "FERPA: When Schools Can't Answer Questions." Education Section. *Daily Press Newport News*, September 17, 2011.

———."Few Local Districts Place Students in K-5 Classrooms." Education Section. *Daily Press Newport News*, September 17, 2011.

Southeastern Louisiana University. "Mortimer Adler: Personal Biography" (accessed October 24, 2011) http://www2.selu.edu/ Academics/Faculty/nadams/educ692/Adler.html.

Usdan, Michael D. "Mayoral Leadership in Education: Current Trends and Future Directions, Mayors and Public Education: The Case for Greater Involvement." *Harvard Educational Review* vol. 76, no. 2 (Summer 2006): 147-152.

Vander Weele, Bill. "School Officials Argue against County Approving Tax Abatements." *Sidney Herald*, August 23, 2011.

Varenne, Hervé. "Educating Ourselves about Education –
 Comprehensively." *Educating Comprehensively: Explorations,
 Possibilities, Challenges.* A special project led by Edmund W.
 Gordon and Hervé Varenne. Volume Two of the Perspectives on
 Comprehensive Education Series (2009) (accessed
 September 3, 2011) http://varenne.tc. columbia.edu/ hv/ edu/
 comprehensive/vol2/vol2-toc.html.

Varenne, Hervé, and Ray McDermott. *Successful Failure: The School
 America Builds.* Boulder, CO: Westview Press, 1998.

Whitlow, Joan. "It's Facebook Money and Newark's Future." *Star-
 Ledger*, October 7, 2011 (accessed October 11, 2011) http://
 blog.nj.com/njv_joan_whitlow/2011/10/ its_facebook_
 money_10_million.html.

ABOUT THE AUTHOR

Patricia Moore Harbour, an educator and certified professional coach, has dedicated her life's work to public education and social change. Her work supports individuals, nonprofit organizations, school districts, communities, and professionals to build collaborative partnerships. She coaches individuals, teams, and groups to bring their personal and professional best into their own lives and the lives of others. She is committed to how we, citizens young and senior, can increase our capacity to live and work together from the strengths of our common humanity.

Harbour's professional experiences include: associate of the Charles F. Kettering Foundation, CEO/president of the Harbour Center for Quality Education LLC, and founder of Healing the Heart of Diversity, a Fetzer Institute initiative. As a federal government employee, she served as executive director for the United States Federal Observances for the International Year of the Child; Special Assistant to the Secretary of Health, Education, and Welfare; and Special Assistant to the US Commissioner of Education. She has served in many capacities in public education, including classroom teacher, principal, and assistant superintendent. Her education, training, and social change leadership work has taken her to England, Japan, South Africa, and West Africa.

Her publications include: "Communities: A Resource—Broadening the Definition of Education," in *Connections*

(Kettering Foundation, 2011); "What's Changed? Are Citizens Reestablishing Education Ownership?" in *Connections* (Kettering Foundation, 2009); "An Educator's Commentary," in *Emotional Development and Emotional Intelligence*, edited by Salovey & Sluyter; and "A Strategy for Social Change in Diversity Practice," in Diversity Central, an online publication. Harbour's work is cited in a number of publications, including Brookfield and Preskill, *Discussion as a Way of Teaching: Tools and Techniques for Democratic Classrooms* and E. Dorian *Gadsden's Resolving the Dilemma*.

Harbour earned a Doctorate of Education Administration and Policy Studies from the George Peabody College of Education at Vanderbilt University. She conducts her work through public speaking, facilitation, training seminars, and professional coaching. She emphasizes ownership and responsibility for individual and collective outcomes. Her goal is that clients build an internal capacity to continue moving forward independently.

> To contact Pat Harbour, send an e-mail to
> pharbour_communityeducators@yahoo.com